Music 7–11

Music is an area of the curriculum which teachers often feel apprehensive about. This book attempts to dispel the myth that to teach music effectively a teacher has to be an accomplished musician. It provides teachers with the opportunity to develop the subject knowledge and the confidence needed to deliver enjoyable and valuable music lessons. It does this by encouraging practical engagement with the subject through making and listening to music, reflecting on experiences and sharing views.

Sarah Hennessy is currently Lecturer in Music Education at Exeter University, prior to which she practised as a classroom and then an advisory teacher of music.

Curriculum in primary practice series
General editor: Clive Carré

The Curriculum in primary practice series is aimed at students and qualified teachers looking to improve their practice within the context of the National Curriculum. The large format, easy to use texts are interactive, encouraging teachers to engage in professional development as they read. Each contains:

- Summaries of essential research
- Activities for individual and group use

While all primary teachers will find these books useful, they are designed with the needs of teachers of the 7 to 11 age group particularly in mind.

Other titles in this series include:

Science 7–11
Clive Carré and Carrie Ovens

Religious Education 7–11
Terence Copley

Forthcoming titles in this series in 1995:

English 7–11
David Wray

Music 7–11

Developing primary teaching skills

Sarah Hennessy

London and New York

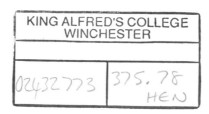
First published 1995
by Routledge
11 New Fetter Lane, London EC4P 4EE

Simultaneously published in the USA and Canada
by Routledge
29 West 35th Street, New York, NY 10001

© 1995 Sarah Hennessy

Typeset in Palatino by Solidus (Bristol) Limited
Printed and bound in Great Britain by
Clays Ltd, St. Ives PLC

British Library Cataloguing in Publication Data
A catalogue record for this book is available from the British Library

Library of Congress Cataloging in Publication Data
A catalogue record for this book has been requested

ISBN 0–415–10558–7

Contents

Acknowledgements

Many of the teaching activities described in this book derive from the practice of music teachers I have worked with. It is difficult to attribute ideas to particular authors as ideas are freely shared and handed on through workshops; this, therefore, is by way of a general 'thankyou' for all that I have learned from them. However I would like to acknowledge the ideas of Wolfgang Hartmann (for activities 5.2 and 5.3) whose workshops for teachers organised by the Orff Society are an inspiration. The 'Habanera' idea I first came across in a workshop led by Joan Arnold.

My thanks go to Wendy Reynolds and the children in her class at Sampford Peverell Primary School in Devon, and John Saunders who photographed them; also the children at Stoke Hill Middle School in Exeter, photographed by Phil Head.

The photograph of the Kokuma Performing Arts workshop was taken by Karam Ram.

Introduction

This book is for all those primary teachers who would like to teach music to their class. Its purpose is to provide, with some theoretical support, practical guidance to increasing knowledge of music and in developing approaches to its teaching.

It is now fairly well recognised that many teachers are unsure of their ability to teach music. Research by Wragg, Bennett and Carré (1989) revealed that, in their sample of 901 primary teachers, music and design and technology were the subjects non-specialists felt least competent to teach in the light of their existing subject knowledge.

It seems probable that this has been largely a result of a long-held and generally unchallenged view that music can and should only be taught by formally trained 'musicians'. As long as music in education was seen as being only concerned with learning the skills to perform, there was little possibility that other teachers could or would feel confident to engage with the subject. It also has to be said that those with the 'gift' were not too convinced of how such teachers could be involved. However, in recent years a combination of factors have changed this situation:

- Fewer and fewer schools have been in a position to employ a 'floating' specialist.
- It has become increasingly difficult (and perhaps undesirable) for specialists to fulfil both the role of class teacher and of music teacher for other classes.
- Amongst music educationalists themselves there has been a strong lobby for music to be treated in the same way as all other subjects in primary school.
- The advent of GCSE has made new and challenging demands on the traditional skills of music teachers, particularly with regard to composing, which now has equal status with performing and listening. (This shift towards a more creative and practical curriculum in secondary schools provided the much-needed impetus for primary schools to establish and develop similar aims. Music education is now much closer in its aims and objectives to those of the other arts in the curriculum. Learning in and through the arts is developed

through practical, creative and critical engagement.)

- In moving away from the notion of music teacher as director/performer/trainer/conductor, new approaches have been explored which make music-making not only more accessible to young children, but also to their teachers.
- Despite many concerns and reservations about the National Curriculum as a whole, the music education community has welcomed the impetus it has provided. Schools are now expected to provide continuity of experience and coherence in music for all children.

It would be wrong to suggest that no creative music-making existed prior to these recent developments. The work of (amongst others) Carl Orff in the 1950s and 1960s and John Paynter in the 1970s underpins much of current thinking and practice; but it has taken economic and legislative action to effect change in the education community as a whole. A noisy revolution has begun, and will continue, to make music a creative art for all. Music in education must be taught as a living art; not as museum or tourist art, as it has sometimes appeared.

For many music teachers, the inclusion of composing and increased emphasis on listening are relatively new, even daunting, aspects to the curriculum. They may never, for instance, have composed or improvised themselves, let alone taught others to do so; but their experience and skills enable them to recognise and appreciate the musical possibilities, to understand the underlying concepts and to assimilate new ideas more rapidly than teachers who are inexperienced or unconfident in teaching or making music. I suspect that many of the latter are rather tired of being told that the ability to read music and play the piano is not necessarily relevant to teaching music effectively. It might be easy for me, in hindsight, to see the limitations of staff notation, but not so easy for those who have never learned it to set aside their anxieties or scepticism. Teachers will only be convinced of the arguments through their own experience of making music and of seeing children music-making as a direct result of their own teaching; this book seeks to provide some of that experience.

WHO CAN TEACH MUSIC?

It is obvious that teachers teach best what they know well and value. Alexander in *Primary Teaching* puts this clearly:

1   What teachers do not adequately understand they are unlikely to teach well.
2   What teachers do not value they are unlikely to teach well.
3   What teachers do not understand they are unlikely to value.

(1984:73)

For this reason, this book attempts to do more than present teaching materials and practical advice. I hope that it will act as a guide, resource and support for teachers wanting to further their subject knowledge so that they might become more independent and able to contribute to the development of music in their schools.

The most effective way of using this book will be in the context of in-service workshops in school. There are three audiences:

- teachers with music teaching experience
- teachers with little or none
- student teachers

These groups are interdependent with regard to the way their skills, knowledge and understanding of teaching and of teaching music can be shared and developed. Those in the first group are particularly significant in their role as potential curriculum leaders and consultants. In my experience, non-specialists are often most anxious about the prospect of singing and other performing skills; they are unsure of their ability to reproduce rhythms or melodies accurately. Those teachers who do have some experience, in this sometimes over-emphasised aspect of music teaching, need to do two things:

1   Encourage their colleagues to rediscover and develop these skills in themselves in a way which values a range of quality.
2   Help them to realise the possibilities for providing all kinds of music learning without the need to be an accomplished performer.

They should be sensitive to the particular interests, abilities and needs of individuals, and be familiar with the particular school context.

I am well aware that many schools may not have anyone in this first group, but I am also fairly sure that it is unusual for there to be no one who does not have some practical experience in music, be it elementary recorder playing, singing, three-chord guitar playing, or dancing. Perhaps the first task the staff should undertake is an audit of skills and experience 'hidden' amongst the staff. I have come across many teachers who have kept secret their playing skills, through a feeling either that they are not good enough or that, if made public, they will be lumbered with taking on responsibility for music: assemblies, hymn practice, Christmas, etc. Even where there is a specialist, the teaching of music should never be the exclusive responsibility of one teacher – this is rare in other subjects, and perpetuates the extra-specialism and elitism surrounding music.

All teachers can include music in their classrooms, but I do not want to pretend that it can be done without some work. Music teaching does demand that teachers can make and listen to music with enough confidence and understanding to develop these qualities in their pupils; but this should not imply that the teacher needs a wonderful singing voice or sophisticated instrumental skills. Of course you cannot teach a song without singing it, or teach a rhythm without sounding or showing it; but your own performance limitations should not prevent you from providing worthwhile musical experiences for your pupils; nor should they prevent us from appreciating the quality of what they do and how they respond. All musicians, however accomplished, live with the realisation that (apart from those who have great aptitude, opportunity and commitment) our technical abilities may often fall short of what we hear in our heads. As experience and understanding develop, our knowledge of and response to music will continue to deepen, long after our performing skills have peaked.

Music arises from ordinary activity that we all share: vocalising, moving, hearing, feeling, imagining, thinking; and on elements that we all use and learn to recognise within these activities: rhythm, pitch, dynamics, speed, etc. The early stages of musical development in school can and should be the responsibility of those who know their children best, i.e. class teachers. In this way, 'music takes its place as part of the whole primary curriculum. Children and teachers make day-to-day links between work in music and other curriculum areas . . . and . . . class teachers will know their pupils' musical progress at first hand' (Mills 1991:2).

HOW TO USE THIS BOOK

It is unlikely that anyone without experience or knowledge could learn how to teach music from reading a book, however careful the author was in avoiding jargon and staff notation. Making the sounds, responding through listening and moving, and sharing ideas and feelings about the music are the ways in which we come to learn the necessary skills, knowledge and understanding. This is quite obvious when we are talking about children's learning in music; why should it be any different for us? The main differences are in the knowledge that teachers are already experienced learners and teachers; and in the recognition of the sizeable repertoire of music all have absorbed and come to know through their lives. Otherwise it seems clear that we need to learn in music through the same processes that we advocate for children, i.e. composing, performing and listening.

This is, therefore, very much a book for teachers to work with together, in a workshop setting, ideally led by a colleague with some music-making or teaching experience. Everyone should take turns in leading an activity or discussion, with expertise being drawn upon and shared where appropriate. Because of my decision to exclude notated examples I have often had to use rather hackneyed examples of songs or pieces. These should be supplemented with other material in the school's repertoire or new pieces contributed by the participants (many published resources now come with a tape so that new repertoire can be learned by everyone). What is important about my choices is how they reflect or illustrate particular musical concepts, techniques or teaching styles. Work through my example first and then suggest others which could provide the same experience, a variant or an extension to the activity.

Music demands good quality concentration and attention, so keep sessions fairly short, especially if they are planned for after school. Sixty to ninety minutes should be sufficient time for the group to go through things more than once and to talk. One unit might provide material for three or four workshops, perhaps more. If using a training day, I would advocate a single two- to three-hour session with a break, as anyone who has little experience of music-making will tire.

Depending on the experience and confidence of individuals, some agreed follow-up should be negotiated. Everyone needs to take ideas straight into their classrooms and try them out with their own children. A system of recording what you attempt will help you to reflect on your and the children's learning as well as provide feedback for the next workshop. Written notes, audio or video tape could be used.

For some teachers the follow-up may be simply to introduce a ten-minute session for rhythm games two or three times a week; for others it may be incorporating some instrumental work into singing sessions, or developing a small composition project.

The book also aims to help the workshop leader find an approach and style which make the subject knowledge accessible and demystify some of the jargon. Because of sometimes deep anxieties felt by colleagues about teaching music, the leader needs to be sympathetic, patient, encouraging and not over-critical. An atmosphere of trust is essential.

For teachers working on their own, the book should act as a stimulus for challenging perceptions and encouraging them to learn alongside their pupils, some of whom may already have performance skills that can be exploited for everyone's benefit. Many schools already encourage schemes whereby older children help the youngest children with reading. Why not extend this idea to teaching songs and rhythm games? Children can be music consultants!

As I have implied already, this book will not change practice on its own, but I hope that it will help in going beneath the surface of the subject knowledge, lack of which prevents independent thought and action. Four of the six units are centred around musical elements: Pulse and rhythm, Pitch and melody, Form, and Texture. I have included a unit on listening as there are activities and issues which, I feel, can be considered more effectively in this way. Within each unit the activities generally progress from elementary or introductory activities through to more advanced and extended ones. Some should occupy no more than five or ten minutes at any one time, and should be used as introductory activities. Others might form the basis of a series of lessons. In every case the skills will need practice and concepts will need to be explored in various contexts. Most of the activities are designed for both teacher groups and the classroom; there are a few which are designed to raise issues and stimulate some discussion amongst teachers.

Unit 1

Music curriculum issues

This unit aims to raise a number of issues which have a profound influence on the planning and development of a school's music curriculum. Some of these are concerned with values and guiding principles; others are more mundane, such as how to deal with noise. The values a school places on its music curriculum are, in some measure, expressed through the quality of the environment in which learning takes place, the range and quality of the resources and whether the timetable enables or obstructs musical activity.

Subsequent units explore some of these issues in more detail through practical examples. In the light of increased understanding it might then be necessary to return to this unit for some reconsideration.

WHY TEACH MUSIC?

'Because the National Curriculum demands it' would be the easy but rather bleak answer. Needless to say, legislation will not, in the short term, change the way people think and feel. Unless we appreciate the value of a subject for ourselves, it is always going to struggle for recognition and status in our individual classrooms.

The following two activities are designed to raise some awareness of attitudes and values.

 ACTIVITY 1.1

Brainstorm the skills, knowledge and understanding which are developed through and by music-making and listening.

Music must first be valued for itself and then for how it might promote and develop skills that are shared by other spheres of learning and experience. At the same time, subjects do not exist in isolation from each other and what we discover through music about the world and our relationship to it develops our consciousness as a whole – not just the 'musical' bit (if there is such a thing). In *Music, Mind and Education*, Swanwick writes: 'it is the *special* function of art, to strengthen, to extend, to illuminate, to transform, and, ultimately, to make life worth living, more "like life"' (1988:50).

ACTIVITY 1.2

Recall and describe, to a partner in the group, a musical event or experience which was particularly exciting, dramatic, significant – a peak experience. What made it so? (The music itself, the people you were with, the occasion . . .?)

It is very rare to find anyone who does not enjoy listening and responding to music, and therefore everyone may be described as being musical in its broadest sense. The sticking point for most people (and this can include children) is in performance or 'joining in'. For some people the inhibitors begin to develop in childhood and this may be largely the result of reactions and comments (even looks) made by teachers to their music-making efforts. The message that making music is only for those who show special aptitude can be transmitted at an early age, and stick; being unmusical is a biological state for which education cannot compensate. An emphasis on performance and its related skills is bound to reinforce this view – e.g. only those who can sing in tune or clap a rhythm accurately at a certain age (as young as seven years old, sometimes) are selected to sing in the choir or to learn to play an instrument. It is the only subject in the primary curriculum which can exercise such overt selection unchallenged by parents and educationalists.

Devising a curriculum which aims to nurture involvement in and appreciation of music in every child is bound to cause some rethinking about values as well as content.

Children's music suffers from being heard as poorly executed adult music, rather than understood and appreciated in the way that children's art-making or writing seem to be. This is not to deny the importance of teaching and learning musical technique, but to suggest that we have been too ready to neglect the development of such skills in the majority in the face of a quite small minority who show special aptitude. Children's music-making must be valued for itself and to do this we need to involve ourselves in the practical, noisy, exhilarating business of making music with children and to learn to recognise, through listening, what they have learned and what might follow.

ACTIVITY 1.3

In two separate groups write down ten statements which express the views of the group with regard to the aims of music education in your school. Give due consideration to cross-curricular issues such as equal opportunities, special needs and cultural diversity. The final list of statements needs to be agreed by everyone. Then bring the groups together and negotiate a final set of ten statements from the two lists.

This process will help in the sharing of perceptions, values and differences. Policy statements and curriculum guidelines will only be effective if everyone has a hand in their creation. The discussion will also allow teachers to look at their current practice and identify in-service needs and wants. There is little point in drawing up a set of policy statements that can only be carried out by a full-time music specialist, though there may be some statements which need specialist teaching. Staffing, resourcing, accommodation and timetabling issues can then be clearly addressed. Short-, medium- and long-term aims may now be discussed.

With increased experience and understanding as a result of professional development, these statements will undoubtedly change, but they should provide an initial base for such development.

Music in the National Curriculum (DES 1992) provides some guidelines for planning and assessing music learning. The fundamental activities of composing, performing and listening are acknowledged in the names of the attainment targets and, for assessment purposes, weighted two-to-one in favour of AT1:

AT 1: Performing and composing

AT 2: Listening and appraising.

It is important to remember that this document is an attempt to simplify the assessment of what is a highly complex learning process. Such a document cannot adequately show the interactive and interdependent nature of these activities; what it can do is deconstruct some of the processes that lead to progression in music learning.

The practical experience offered in this book should help teachers understand these processes and as a result make their own planning, teaching and assessment more coherent. In-service in whatever guise is only successful if at the end of the programme teachers can continue with some measure of independence. When they have used these materials or ideas they should then be able to go on to find or devise others which reinforce, develop and enrich the learning.

ASSESSMENT

Whilst music education was mainly concerned with performing, assessment was commonly seen as measuring technique: singing or playing in tune, keeping in time, reading notation and aural skills. Musicality was considered to be too subjective and therefore not appropriate for assessment, as everyone's response to a piece of music would be bound to be coloured by their own experience and taste. 'Gut feelings' or intuition have tended to be the way teachers have finally arrived at a view about the quality or effectiveness of musical outcomes, whether performed or composed.

With a new emphasis on composing, a different and more all-encompassing approach to assessment needs to be addressed. Musical behaviour is seen not only when children perform, it is also seen, for instance, when they explore the sounds they can produce on a suspended cymbal, improvise a musical conversation with a friend on a Gato drum, dance, describe their reaction to a piece of music they have listened to, and so on.

Assessment in music is achieved through:

- listening critically to how and what children perform and compose
- listening to and observing how children go about their music-making
- discussing with children their ideas and intentions
- listening to children's assessments of their own and other music
- listening, observing and reading how children respond when listening to music through other media such as visual art, dance, drama, poetry, etc.

All of these may be integrated into the process of composing. It is here that control of sound is made evident; the ability to listen attentively is proved; musical influences, knowledge of form and style are exploited; and musical imagination can show itself.

In 'Understanding Children's Musical Understanding', Glover (1990) suggests that we need to take 'the widest possible view'. In a project involving student teachers and pupils at a junior school, Glover set out to investigate developmental patterns of children's music-making. She arrived at some valuable conclusions about the conditions necessary to gain such insight. These are paraphrased here:

- A child must be 'tracked', over time, through a programme of work which should include individual as well as group work. 'The teacher needs to live with the music.'
- Some of the tasks that children engage in should be uncommissioned, for 'they reveal a great deal about their understanding of . . . what music is and can do'.
- Tasks should allow for interaction between related activities (e.g. exploration – composition – performing – performing to different audiences).
- Consideration should be given to the extent to which a composition shows what has been achieved intuitively and what has been consciously worked on.
- A range of approaches should be used to gather evidence: taking part in an improvisation, being shown how to play a composition, talking with a child about their music, and so on.

It is important to remember that this kind of understanding needs to develop over time and needs practice and support. Glover is, however, quite sure that class teachers can acquire the habit of trying to understand children's work in music, and that once they do 'the problems of how to chart development and "match" it in planning for progression begin to dissolve'.

I would hope that through working with the ideas in this book, teachers will begin to develop their own musical understanding in a quite conscious way, so that they might then recognise the evidence of it in their children. Our understanding is not only developed by our own efforts but by what we learn from the efforts of others; and by this I mean children as well as adults.

PERFORMING: SINGING AND PLAYING

Singing is a ubiquitous feature of primary school culture. It is unquestionably seen as 'a good thing', even in schools where the quality of singing is poor and enthusiasm is minimal amongst children and teachers. Playing instruments raises issues of equal opportunity, access, cost, management and noise – whether we are thinking of classroom percussion, steel pans, electronic keyboards, guitars or orchestral instruments.

Activity 1.4 invites you to carry out a survey or audit of what goes on in your school, and may provide an opportunity for discussion towards developing policy.

 ACTIVITY 1.4

- In your school, when and how does singing happen?
- How often and which members of staff are involved in the singing?
- Are there opportunities for solo or small group singing?
- Who chooses the songs and how do you learn new ones?
- How are songs accompanied?
- Would you describe the repertoire as musically varied?
- Is there a conscious effort to choose songs from different times and cultures?
- Are songs chosen to develop vocal technique and therefore to suit vocal maturity?
- Does the school enjoy singing?
- If there is a school choir, are children auditioned or can anyone join?

This is not an exhaustive list but should help to focus on the nature, content and quality of singing in your school. Singing can be used for all kinds of learning in music; using the voice as another sound-maker when composing adds enormously to the range of sounds, particularly as percussion instruments cannot sustain sounds as the voice can. It is through the voice that we gain the most profound understanding of the relationship between listening and sounding.

Playing instruments

- How many children have regular opportunities to play instruments in school, including percussion?
- Do all classes have access to instruments for music lessons?
- How many classrooms include a music 'corner' or work-station for individual or small group work?
- What proportion of children have instrumental tuition in school or privately?
- How are children chosen for instrumental tuition?
- What instruments are on offer? Are they only the orchestral ones?
- What information is given to parents about their role in supporting this kind of learning?
- What is the drop-out rate?

- How are these children's skills integrated into class music lessons?
- What provision is made for children who are learning instruments to play together?

These are some of the questions that need to be considered. The context in which instrumental teaching is provided has changed dramatically with the demise of centrally funded LEA services. Every school must now devise its own policy and manage it in the light of local circumstances. Much may be lost if schools do not give some attention to this aspect of the music curriculum, and where provision may have been poor in the past there is now the opportunity to improve it.

The traditional one-to-one teaching approach is only one of several ways to use the expertise of a visiting tutor. Group tuition, taking part in class music lessons, improvising and composing with children, and directing ensembles are ways in which specialists can become a more integral part of the curriculum.

It is probably the only subject in which a significant minority of children can have such different experience and skills to those of the majority; but it should be remembered that learning to play an instrument does not automatically include developing composing or even listening skills. Many instrumental teachers are now working to redress this imbalance and looking for ways to develop their specialist role in schools.

NOTATION

Teaching notation needs to have purpose and meaning. It should, in the first instance, arise out of a need that the music-maker identifies. It can have several different purposes:

- To help us remember – as an *aide-mémoire* – we may just write down an outline, important moments, or complicated passages.
- To communicate our music for others to play; in which case they need to understand our language.
- To give everyone a plan (score) of what happens. Each player can see how their part fits into the whole. This is useful for a conductor, if there is one.
- To help in the refining and rehearsing process. The composer can 'tinker' with the piece and refer to particular sections in rehearsal. Individual players or groups can take their part away to practice.
- To enable the music-makers to experiment and discover different interpretations of the same score. It is not usually possible or desirable for the written music to dictate exactly how the music should be performed. (How loud is loud?)
- To give children (in the context of the wider curriculum) an opportunity to explore the nature of visual symbols and their power to communicate meaning.

Simple rhythmic or melodic patterns can be easily translated into all sorts of visual patterns. Almost anything can be used, given the space: shoes, children themselves, bricks, graphic symbols, etc. The most easily understood ideas tend to be able to show relationships of time within the patterns in a simple way. Some will only work for short, simple patterns. Staff notation is quite economical and accurate in representing certain kinds of rhythm, which is why it has survived for quite a long time.

Year 5 children devised this graphic score to record their group composition

Being able to read music does not mean that one is automatically more musical. Literacy gives access to a large and culturally significant literature for music-making, but it can also act as a great inhibitor to spontaneity, responsiveness and listening in those who have been taught to rely on it.

A balance needs to be struck, especially in the primary curriculum, between the view that 'real' music is notated music and the opposite view that staff notation is entirely unimportant. The National Curriculum, sensibly, does not insist on all children being taught only staff notation. It refers to graphic scores, symbols and notations (the plural is significant). Even at Key Stage 3, references to staff notation are often presented alongside suggested alternatives.

For teachers it is an obvious advantage for learning new material, but much of the song repertoire we use is more likely to have been learned from hearing and joining in (with other teachers, in workshops, with tapes or broadcasts).

The principles of notating simple melodies and rhythm patterns are dealt with in numerous curriculum materials and with help from someone who knows the basics they can be explained. Exploring and inventing notations with your pupils in the context of music itself should be the first step in understanding their purpose and their limitations.

COMPOSING

Composing, compared to performing, is a slow, messy process which does not lend itself to the teacher-led, whole-class activity that many music teachers have been used to. Many music lessons in the past looked and sounded more like rehearsals than an educative experience; whereas composing is noisy and cannot be directed solely by the teacher.

In school, where learning and productive work are often equated with quiet industry, it can be difficult to accommodate and actively encourage this kind of music-making. Many specialist music teachers have felt just as daunted as everyone else by the idea of teaching composition, and many of us are still at the beginning of our experience and understanding of what is possible.

There is, at present, something of a gap between the majority of music teachers' own education and that which is advocated by the National Curriculum. We must continue to value what teachers already do well and at the same time find ways to develop those skills that have been neglected. The aim is not to produce a nation of professional composers, but to give all children the opportunity to develop musical imagination, insight and understanding. Many teachers who are inexperienced in teaching music will often feel quite confident about providing opportunities, frameworks and guidance for children's creative writing, art work and maybe even drama and dance. Creative work in music needs similar support, and similar approaches. Confidence develops through personal engagement with the medium. In this way the structural and expressive elements which inform the composing process should become more explicit and an understanding of how to guide and advise children will grow.

ACCOMMODATION AND TIMETABLING

It is likely that no single space will fulfil the needs of every music activity.

 ACTIVITY 1.5

Consider where music happens in your school.

Is there a designated room for music, or is it also used for television, special needs, storage, etc? The hall is not necessarily the best space for music, except perhaps for singing; the acoustics may make it very resonant and the space makes it difficult to achieve focus for, say, listening. It would be unwise to generalise, but classrooms will accommodate many music activities with some rearranging of furniture and forewarning of neighbouring classes!

Are there often problems with noise levels? Not all music lessons are noisy, and sometimes non-musical noise levels can be high. Teachers need to be sensitive to each other's needs but also recognise the inevitability of children sometimes needing to make a certain amount of musical 'mess'.

Try also to choose times in the day when there are fewest interruptions (especially when you are focusing on listening). There may be some simple measures which can be taken to cut down noise. Curtains and carpet make a marked difference and, when rooms are being altered or redecorated, insulation, display boards or wall-coverings might also improve things.

I have often noticed that music is allocated a time in the week when both children and teachers may not be at their best for the particular demands of music; Friday afternoons, for instance. It is also the subject which is often squeezed out altogether when there are special events. It might be argued that music monopolises the time-table at times like Christmas, but it is continuity that will facilitate progress, not an experience which bounces between bouts of intense activity and total neglect.

This unit has attempted to raise issues discussion of which should help in the planning and management of teaching music. The most important discussions should be those concerning the shared values and principles which will determine the nature and scope of that music.

Unit 2

Pulse and rhythm

The ability to keep time in music is generally held to be not only a fundamental, but also an 'absolute' skill. Some of us have it, others do not. The lack of this ability is physically and aurally conspicuous, so that we become progressively more inhibited about attempting to take part in music-making. It is, therefore, important to appreciate how this ability can be fostered and developed through simple, manageable, unthreatening and enjoyable activities.

PULSE

All of us have a biological pulse which responds to our changing physical and emotional states. From early childhood we are responding to the regularity of this inner pulse through speech and increasingly coordinated movement. We spend a lot of time with babies and very young children reinforcing these natural, physical characteristics: slow, gentle rocking to calm; quick, lively bouncing to excite. As teachers we can build on this foundation with the knowledge that all children have the ability to develop this sense. What we seek to develop in music is the conscious ability to feel and hear a 'given' pulse to which we move and make sounds. The most common reasons for difficulties with this seem to be a combination of poor listening skills and physical tension, both of which are compounded by the anxiety of 'getting it wrong'. When this happens, enjoyment and learning fly out the window.

The problem for teachers is not so much ineffective teaching, as neglect or avoidance caused by lack of confidence. By trying these simple ideas and sharing those gleaned from each other (and published resources) you should be able to build a sequence of manageable activities which will develop your confidence and that of your children. Hopefully you will discover that all sorts of ideas you have used already under the guise of, say, drama, language or physical education – even those you might associate with just having fun – can be employed. Before embarking on any activity, it might be useful to reflect on all those occasions in school when coordinated, fluent, rhythmic action and sound are present:

- playground games: chanting while clapping, ball bouncing or skipping
- running, dancing, reciting poetry, singing.

There is, quite rightly, great attention given to activities which link language to pulse and rhythm work. Speech rhythms are as important in learning language as the words themselves, and it is certainly a truism for teachers of young children that rhymes and songs develop language. Not surprisingly, music learning is advanced by precisely the same repertoire. These activities naturally stimulate and demand physical movement so that it becomes obvious for us to encourage and extend this relationship in the music curriculum. It is unfortunate that the close links gradually pull apart as we teach older children. The disconnection can be most extreme in those who become physically constrained by the process of learning to play an instrument in the 'classical' tradition. We seem to be discouraged from moving as we play, as this can interfere with the technical demands of playing correctly.

The work of Carl Orff gives the relationships between speech, gesture, movement and music central importance, and many teachers today have applied this to their music teaching. Ulli Jungmair, a lecturer at the Orff Institute in Salzburg, explores these relationships in her practical work with teachers and students:

The expression of language shows itself through the body. The body that has experienced movement builds the foundation for an inner movement when singing and when making music on instruments. Dancing is . . . music being realised through movement, through one's individual rhythm.

(Undated publicity leaflet)

It seems to be generally observed by teachers that girls develop fine motor skills earlier than boys. My inclination is to believe that this is largely a result of nurture rather than nature; and even if I am wrong, there is still a lot we can do to redress it. Through listening, composing and performing, the physical skill can be refined and appreciation of its importance in all musics is developed. Everyone will have picked up some material through their own childhood experience and contact with children: nonsense rhymes, action songs, coordination games, circle games, drama warm-ups. In Activity 2.1 you can begin to recall and share this repertoire.

ACTIVITY 2.1 (teacher/student group)

In pairs, teach each other a rhyme or song that you know well, then to the whole group. Be aware of how you go about teaching it (speed, number of repetitions, etc.). Notice that actions generally keep a regular pulse to hold the whole thing together.

The joy of this type of material is that it is found in children's culture all over the world. There are now many collections of songs and rhymes which include examples from different cultures (see resources). This could spark off an exciting project for a class or even the whole school in which children research and collect material of this kind from amongst themselves, their families and the wider community. Different

generations will be interested to discover the transformations and similarities in particular rhymes and singing games. The findings could be collected and presented in book form, as a visual display, on audio or video tape.

An added refinement is that of internalising words or phrases so that only the actions are performed (but still in time), e.g. 'My hat it had three corners'.

You could also devise an exercise whereby the internalising is more random. Imitate what happens when the car radio is on as you drive through a tunnel, or turning down the volume while the music is playing (are you still in time when the sound comes back?). This kind of activity develops the ability to feel pulse and rhythm through silence, and encourages awareness of our ability to hear music in our head.

a ACTIVITY 2.2

Use a familiar song or rhyme – while the group perform it, the leader makes a hand sign (e.g.'halt' signal) for silent passages. When the sign is cancelled the sounding resumes. A green and a red circle of card (traffic lights) can be used with younger children. This also involves internalising the melody.

With more experienced children it is possible to practise pulse-keeping in a more abstract way, without using words. Be aware that it is much easier to keep time when performing the whole pattern than performing a bit of it.

 ACTIVITY 2.3

Sit in a circle.

1   Lead everyone in tapping a steady beat on knees:

●   ●   ●   ●   ●   ●   ●   ●   ●   ●   etc.

2   Feel the pulse in fours by making the first in each group stronger (perhaps make this a clap – or any body sound: click, stamp; voice sound: la, eek, sss; movement: nod, knee bend, wiggle. Vary for repetitions to avoid monotony or sore hands).

●   ●   ●   ●   ●   ●   ●   ●   ●   ●
1   2   3   4, 1   2   3   4, 1   2   etc.

3   Now change the groupings without stopping the steady pulse, by calling out different numbers:

'four'   'three'   'five'
● ●
1 2 3 4, 1 2 3 4, 1 2 3 4, 1 2 3, 1 2 3, 1 2 3, 1 2 3, 1 2 3 4 5,

The important thing is to keep the pulse steady and regular. Always wait for everyone to be sounding together before giving the next signal.

Try making everyone shut their eyes to improve their listening rather than relying on visual signals.

To introduce silence:

4   Only sound the first beat in each group:

●   ●   ●   ●   ●   ●   ●   ●   ●   ●   ●   ●
1   ,1   ,1

5   Sound all but the first:

●   ●   ●   ●   ●   ●   ●   ●   ●   ●   ●   ●
    2   3   4,   2   3   4,   2   3   4,

It helps to make a silent movement in the gaps to FEEL the pulse (e.g. flap hands in the air). Sustaining the pulse through silence as well as sound is essential to musical development.

Once this kind of activity is well established and has become more or less fluent, move on to more independent work.

ACTIVITY 2.4

Keeping the pulse steady, each person in the circle passes the clap on (like 'pass the parcel').

Vary this exercise by passing other sounds or silent movements round. Change direction sometimes. Clap the pulse round the circle stressing the first in every four (five, three, six, etc.).

All those playing the first beat in the group choose a different sound. Introduce the idea that some particular numbered beats might be a single, silent movement (nod, wave, wiggle, knee-bend, etc.).

In groups of four make up a sound and movement sequence, keeping a steady pulse (robots, machines). Each group adds their sequence to the one before, until the whole class is part of the composition.

Observe that big movements are sometimes difficult to contain within the pulse, especially if it's moving quite fast. You need to be able to repeat the sound or movement a number of times. Give some time for practice before attempting to put it together.

In this way the skill of keeping a pulse through sound and silence is practised and developed but, even at this early stage, you and the children are asked to invent other sounds, to combine and repeat them in sequences, and to perform them as part of a group. Listening, performing and composing are thus integrated.

There are many many activities like these described in published resources for teachers which will enable you to give yourself and your children lots of practice. All these ideas will bear repetition and this is an important feature of all learning in music. Aural and muscle memory build gradually over time and through repetition – LITTLE AND OFTEN is the key. If you or the children make a mess of it, it is probably because you have moved through the activity too quickly, or perhaps set too fast a tempo (speed) for the pulse.

Remember that these kinds of skill development activities need good quality conditions: sitting or standing comfortably, so that everyone can move easily and see the leader; a reasonably controlled environment, quiet and undistracting; and alert and focused attention. Finish the activity with success – don't go on until it begins to fall apart.

Transferring any of these activities onto instruments is appropriate, but the increased volume, playing skills, split focus between listening and watching, and controlling the instrument may be too much for the children and you to handle. Initially you want as few complications as possible.

When you do introduce instruments, select sounds which will complement each other (not just anything you can lay your hands on!) – for crisp, clear sounds use wooden tappers, small drums and shakers – hide the cymbal! If every child is to have an instrument, try to exclude very dominant sounds unless you can be sure that they will be played sensitively.

You need a bit more space to accommodate the playing of instruments, and time to organise. It might be better to plan music sessions with instruments rather more formally than those which can be resourced with our own bodies.

Apart from those activities which involve gestures or actions to accompany the words, keeping time to a piece of music while moving or dancing is another valuable means of development. When you want the focus to be on recognising and feeling the pulse, choose music which simply does this: folk dance music is an excellent resource, tending to be repetitious and with a strong pulse to keep the dancers together.

Activity 2.5 shows how regular pulse-keeping can be used as the basis of a composition.

 ACTIVITY 2.5

In a circle, keep the pulse in sevens (any number will do, but short sequences repeat rather quickly and very long ones are difficult to hang on to).

Each person, secretly, chooses a number between one and seven, and invents a sound to make on that number.

The leader (teacher) keeps a steady pulse speaking it first then, when everyone is 'with' it, tapping on a drum. Ultimately the pulse can be felt and kept by the whole group by listening and concentrating.

As we repeat our sounds a pattern will emerge to create a musical idea:

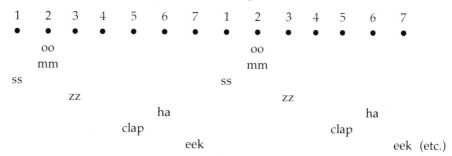

This can form the basis for explorations into patterns of pitch (e.g. use a random selection of chime bars), timbre (e.g. only wood sounds), dynamics (e.g. certain numbers are louder or very soft).

After so many repetitions, play your sound on a different number to change the pattern. Play on two numbers. Try out different 'rules' to manipulate the patterns to achieve particular effects.

Build in silences. Patterns of movement can be created in the same way by moving on chosen numbers. The patterns can be recorded on a score using some kind of graphic notation, e.g.

RHYTHM

Alongside the development of a sense of pulse, we learn to invent or recreate patterns of long and short sounds which fit the pulse. These patterns are RHYTHM. The simplest way to explain the difference between pulse and rhythm is through a song or rhyme.

ACTIVITY 2.6

Choose a partner and face each other (one is A, the other is B). A puts her hands on B's shoulders, while B puts hands on A's waist. All sing or chant this song:

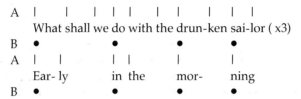

A pats the rhythm of the words on B's shoulders, while B pats the steady pulse on A's waist. Swap over.

Try combining the two individually: walk on the spot for the pulse, clap the rhythm at the same time; or left hand taps pulse, right hand taps rhythm (swap).

Traditional songs and dances tend to have regular rhythm patterns which are easy to identify and copy. This helps us to assimilate them quickly, obviously an important feature of popular music.

When developing a sense of rhythm in children there are three broad stages: joining in, echoing, independence. Young children naturally join in with rhythm and singing, even when the material is entirely new. They learn by imitating and repeating as they listen. This is why the way you 'perform' is so important: when the clapped pattern is presented with energy and clarity, children will copy likewise.

Gradually you can introduce the idea of echoing the pattern or phrase: 'I'll clap a pattern then you clap it back straight away.' This demands more control and the ability to remember the material. Variations on this exercise appear in countless sources (see resources) and children will invent their own games. A quite challenging one is this:

ACTIVITY 2.7

The leader claps a pattern – the group echoes. This continues with a new pattern each time until the leader repeats one.

When the group hear the repeat they must fold their arms instead of clapping.

Leader	Group
| | | |	| | | |
| || || |	| || || |
| | || |	| | || |
| || || |	fold arms

(You might need to write down some patterns as a crib sheet – it takes some practice to hold three or four patterns in your head.)

Answering with a different, but balancing, pattern moves the exercise into improvising and composing.

Leader: ● ● ● ● ● ● ● ●   *Answer:* ● ● ● ● ● ● ● ●
\| \|\| \| \|\|, \| \| \| .\| \| \| \|\| \| , \|\| \|\| \| .

To do this accurately and appropriately needs lots of experience in the first two stages to build up a repertoire of patterns. Nevertheless children should be encouraged to make up their own rhythms (and music of all kinds) right from the beginning. Inventiveness is not a result of skill acquisition, but its breadth and depth are thus developed. When musicians improvise they are not plucking ideas out of the air. Over time they have copied, through playing and listening, existing music, and have absorbed the formulas and patterns which make up a particular style. Improvisations follow learned structures and rules as much as pre-composed music does.

The natural rhythms of our spoken language influence those of our music. A large repertoire of songs and rhymes can be used to develop skill, understanding and inventiveness.

 ACTIVITY 2.8

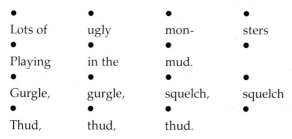

●	●	●	●
Lots of	ugly	mon-	sters
●	●	●	●
Playing	in the	mud.	
●	●	●	●
Gurgle,	gurgle,	squelch,	squelch
●	●	●	●
Thud,	thud,	thud.	

This nonsense rhyme will serve as a starting point for practising rhythms and provide the material for some composition.

1   Learn the rhyme through varied repetitions: whispering, shouting, squeaking, growling, gradually getting louder (quieter, higher, lower), as fast as possible, one word each, etc.
    Keep everyone together by keeping the pulse on your knees.

Note that the pulse goes on through silences (after 'mud' and 'thud'). When everyone is fluent ask them to keep the pulse also. They could repeat Activity 2.6 using this rhyme.

2   Explore ways of arranging and developing the rhythmic material to make it more interesting and substantial. Organise three groups:
speak the rhyme as a round, each group starting two or four beats after the one before

or

build a texture in layers, group A keeping the pulse:

| Mud | mud | mud | mud | etc. |

group B repeating a short phrase:

| Gurgle | gurgle | squelch | squelch | etc. |

group C speaking the whole rhyme:

| Lots of | ug-ly | mon-sters | | etc. |

This basic arrangement can then be expanded and varied to create a more substantial, interesting and technically demanding piece.

Give more structure by each group starting one after the other, e.g. group A do eight 'Mud's (beginning very quietly). Then group B join in with four 'Gurgle gurgle squelch squelch's and finally group C enter saying the whole rhyme twice. Finish as we began with group A fading into the distance.

At any point we can dispense with the words and play the rhythms on body percussion or instruments. Discuss with the group which kinds of sounds to use for each part (low-pitched drums for the pulse, crisp-shakers and tappers for group B, perhaps). Group C can improvise on tuned percussion, sticking to the rhythm of the rhyme but using a limited range of notes, e.g. C D E G A, which gives us the pentatonic scale (see Unit 3).

This activity, which could take several sessions, might serve as a model for groups to find or write their own rhymes and compose pieces derived from the word rhythms.

Many kinds of music in the world are founded on rhythm rather than melody or harmony. Latin American samba, Ghanaian drumming and many other types of music use the idea of repeated patterns which are combined in layers to produce complex interlocking textures. There is melodic material but this may be of secondary importance. The influence of African rhythms has spread through the jazz and pop music of America, and has given us a very different musical world to explore from the traditional folk music of western Europe and the classical repertoire we are most familiar with.

The main features of these rhythms are syncopation and cross-rhythms where the strong beats of the pattern do not coincide with the strong pulses. Listen to any piece of ragtime (e.g. 'The Entertainer' by Scott Joplin) or reggae. Both these styles are characterised by particular rhythmic formulas which are repetitive and quite simple to identify.

ACTIVITY 2.9

Listen to the first section of 'The Entertainer' (other pieces will do just as well, but this is probably the best known). The bass line accompaniment, in the left hand, plays a steady 'vamp', on the beat. The right hand plays the melody, which has a strong, repeated rhythm. The important, emphasised notes fall between the left-hand chords.

Try putting the two together in a group. One group claps the bass line or uses a combination of two sounds (e.g. lap clap lap clap). The other group clap the right-hand part. They could, alternatively, invent a spoken version using real words or nonsense syllables: 'da da dee da dee da dee da', like scat singers use in jazz. It should also be possible to devise a dance routine where the feet tap out the pattern. Swap the groups over so that the bass line keepers don't get worn out.

Despite the seeming predominance of rock and pop music in our lives, much of the repertoire in schools does not reflect this, nor do those who learn to play instruments in the conven-

Musicians from Kokuma Performing Arts working with children on rhythm

tional way explore these styles very much. As a result there is often a lack of skill and confidence in responding with physical ease and fluency to music that is mainly or wholly rhythmic. It is worth reflecting on the thought that most musical styles which use complex interlockings and cross-rhythms tend to be oral, not literary traditions. European music would have developed very differently without notation.

Moving, dancing and clapping to all kinds of music will encourage a less inhibited response. There are now many professional musicians and dancers offering workshops and residencies in schools to give children a 'live', practical experience of particular styles. This kind of experience can provide support for and enhancement of the whole curriculum, as well as in-service for teachers.

ACTIVITY 2.10

Here is a simple example of a piece of music using the idea of rhythm layers. Representing rhythm patterns in this way can help in an understanding of how the complex patterns found in many African musical traditions are organised.

On a board or large sheet of paper write:

(a) ① 2 3 ④ ⑤ 6 7 ⑧ ① 2 3 ④ ⑤ 6 7 ⑧
(b) 1 ② ③ 4 5 ⑥ ⑦ ⑧ 1 ② ③ 4 5 ⑥ ⑦ ⑧
(c) 1 ② 3 ④ 5 ⑥ 7 ⑧ 1 ② 3 ④ 5 ⑥ 7 ⑧
(d) ① 2 ③ 4 ⑤ 6 ⑦ 8 ① 2 ③ 4 ⑤ 6 ⑦ 8
(As many layers as you can handle!)

Make one row the steady pulse – in this case row (d). The circled numbers are clapped and the other numbers are silent (felt).

Everyone practises each row until it is accurate and steady. Start with a slow count, but eventually it should rattle along quite quickly. At speed you become more aware of the interlocking effects.

Once the class/group are familiar with the patterns, divide them into groups (make sure there is a reasonable ability mix in each). Each group then plays one row over and over, so that all the patterns are sounding together. With everyone clapping it might be difficult to identify each pattern, so transfer onto percussion instruments when everyone is reasonably fluent. The steady pulse should be kept on low-pitched drums (if there is only one, use it for one player who is able to play solo). Graduate the pitch range of each group's instruments and also choose similar timbres e.g.:

row (d) low drums
row (c) claves and wood blocks (avoid wooden beaters – they can be ear-splitting)
row (b) bongos and small drums played with hands
row (a) shakers and cabasa

In both Ghana and Brazil, cow bells, agogo bells and scrapers (guiro) are also used. Latin American percussion is largely derived from African instruments, the main difference being that in the former, materials include metal and plastic which produce a much louder, brighter sound.

This way of building a rhythmic texture is used in some computer programmes (such as RhythmBox). The screen displays a grid, each square of which represents a unit of time. You compose rhythm patterns by 'clicking on' chosen squares. Different sounds can be used for different rows in the grid, and the tempo can be varied.

Exploring and learning to play in such musical styles is, of course, rewarding in itself, but will also develop a strong sense of rhythm which is felt as well as heard. It is impossible to be still when playing or listening, and the more opportunities that can be found for dancing the better.

In developmental terms we want to be able to recognise, reproduce and invent increasingly complex and more unexpected patterns of sound and silence. Not only do the rhythms themselves become more demanding, but also the combining of patterns played simultaneously needs to be explored. Rhythms that are more fragmented, less repetitive, include lots of silence and 'off beats' (syncopation) are more difficult to learn and perform. Very slow or very fast-moving rhythms make particular demands on the ability to control and physically articulate them. Speaking or singing the rhythm is very useful. In oral music traditions musicians develop a way of speaking the rhythm for teaching and learning. Tabla players learn and memorise the highly complex patterns in Indian classical music in this way, each syllable representing a particular drum stroke, e.g.:

1	2	3	4	5	6	7	8	1
dha	ge	na	tin	na	ka	dhin	–	dha, etc.

Music traditions in other parts of the world adopt similar practices. In the European classical tradition over a few hundred years a system of notation has developed. Most people who learn classical music in Europe learn from staff notation, not by listening and imitating. This 'note-bound' approach can lead to a rather rigid, unresponsive attitude to music-making. It also makes it difficult for musicians to move freely between different styles and traditions. Teachers need to find ways of establishing a feeling for rhythm, before teaching the visual symbols that represent it. Keeping time and developing a sense of rhythm needs time; time to listen, and translate what we hear into movement and sound, and time to practise quick responses and muscle memory for accuracy, fluency and stamina. Listening to and identifying rhythm patterns in pieces of music develop a bank of material to use in improvising and composing. Playing, singing and dancing in a wide variety of styles will nurture skill, understanding and appreciation.

Unit 3

Pitch and melody

Like the sense of pulse and rhythm, singing or playing 'in tune' is seen as an uncompromising ability. 'Good' intonation is central to the development of all singing and playing, except of course for instruments like the piano, where the tuning is prepared. We are far less able, it seems, to tolerate the sound of a beginner violinist playing slightly out of tune than the inaccuracy of perspective in an inexperienced painter.

PITCH

Hearing and reproducing pitched sounds is the ability which enables us to remember, perform and create melody, and this can be developed and improved through practical, active engagement. The most effective, productive and economical way to develop this ability is through the voice. Again, as with rhythm, we all use and hear pitch movement in speech (intonation or inflection).

 ACTIVITY 3.1

Have a conversation with a partner – this could be an extract from a book or play script, or improvised. Try speaking your words in different ways, e.g. on a mono-tone; exaggerating the ups and downs; in a depressed, excited or puzzled mood. Then have a conversation (perhaps an argument) in which there are no meaningful words but the meaning is conveyed by the inflection of your voices. You could use numbers (count up to one hundred), or nursery rhymes.

Obviously pitch is not the only element that changes, but it is probably the most important in conveying feeling and mood. Higher pitch may give a feeling of tension, urgency, excitement, being out of control, or anger; whereas lower pitch gives a sense of calmness, control, solemnity or power. Activity 3.2 provides an opportunity for everyone to focus simply on sound.

 ACTIVITY 3.2

In your ordinary speaking voice, say 'Hello' (or any simple greeting word), one at a time around the circle. How does the sound change from one voice to the next? There may be several answers: some are louder (bigger), lower, quicker, etc. Tease out the words which describe dynamics (loud and soft), pitch (high and low), and duration (long and short).

These describe the three most fundamental ways in which a single sound can be changed. Finding and developing a common language which describes what we hear is very important. It will provide a means, alongside others such as using notations or performing, of assessing listening skills. In group composing it also enables everyone to share and clarify their ideas. Young children use the words 'high' and 'loud', and 'low' and 'quiet' interchangably (it doesn't help that we talk about high and low volume). The distinctions need to be made through sounding, listening and describing.

Take each element and, round the circle, vocalise their extremes. Start with pitch: each person says either 'high' in a high voice or 'low' in a low voice, alternately. Later do the same with 'loud' and 'soft'; and 'long' and 'short'.

Many children are unsure of how the voice works, and this is a good moment to focus on this (a link with science might be possible). Also it is common to find boys in their junior years neglecting the higher end of their pitch range. This seems to be a result of social pressure to emulate 'manly' voices, often several years before the voice breaks. There is a possibility that there are many boys with perfectly good singing voices who, perhaps quite unconsciously, turn themselves into 'growlers' by trying to sing only on their lowest notes. The reverse of this may be true in some girls, although singing seems to be far more acceptable amongst girls (more of this later!).

With the pitch exercise encourage extremes. Year 1 and 2 children might need some extra illustration (e.g. mice and bears) to realise the sounds.

 ACTIVITY 3.3

Place two fingers on the nobbly bit at the front of your neck, and swallow. It should move up and down. This is your voice box (larynx). Now do the high/low exercise individually and feel what happens. In this way children may realise that the voice is something tangible over which they have real control and that, just like other muscles, it can be exercised and developed.

With the 'loud' and 'soft' exercise, the use of energy to push out the air, exaggerating the mouth movements, even the whole body movement can be noted and discussed. How do singers, for instance, learn to make such a big sound? (An opportunity here to invite a parent or friend with a trained voice to come in and demonstrate.)

With the 'long' and 'short' exercise, it is breath control that is the focus. Controlling volume, sustaining long notes, and developing good tone are all dependent on breathing.

ACTIVITY 3.4

Stand with feet slightly apart in an upright but relaxed posture (not a ramrod!). Take some deep breaths slowly in, on a count of three, and out, on a count of three. The count for breathing out can gradually be increased. The crucial factor is expanding the rib cage, not lifting your shoulders up to your ears. Children can feel this by standing in a circle facing the back of the child to their right. Put both hands on the ribs of the person in front and everyone can feel the rib cage expanding and contracting as they all breathe. (If everyone gets too tickly and giggly, abandon and use yourself as the example.)

Finding out about breathing

Take a breath in; hum on any single note and walk slowly and steadily round the room stopping wherever you are when the sound runs out. The more energy that is used in moving, the less you will have for humming. Try humming loudly or very quietly. Lots of variations and developments of this basic exercise can be invented.

They need to be simple, fairly short, achievable and fun. One or two at the start of a singing session will contribute to the quality of performance.

NB: Too many breathing exercises may produce dizziness.

It is important to remember that vocal flexibility and range take a long time to develop and mature. Professional singers often don't reach their peak until well into their thirties. There are great individual variations as well as marked differences in the rate of development between male and female voices. Many adults believe that there is something called 'tone-deafness'. This condition allows lots of people to opt out of music-making in general and singing in particular. In reality this condition is incredibly rare (something like one in a million), if it exists at all. If someone was truly tone deaf they would speak on a monotone and be unable to identify any pitch variation in what they heard.

What is a much more common condition is difficulty in pitching the voice accurately when singing with others, or 'finding' your singing voice. Lack of practice, praise and confidence is enough to convince anyone that they cannot sing. This conviction can begin to develop in primary school; consequently it is at this stage that most can be done to prevent a collapse in confidence. The best possible environment for singing to be nurtured is one in which everybody sings – not just those with wonderful voices, but *everyone*. Male teachers in primary schools can sometimes feel inhibited about singing because their voices are pitched lower than women's and children's. Children don't find this a problem, they will naturally sing in their own range. It is very important that children hear and see men singing, as this will help to dispel the idea that singing is a female preserve. It is difficult to understand how this idea is turned on its head in the world of pop music, where there are far more male singing stars than female ones.

Some of the difficulty of encouraging boys to sing can be addressed through the repertoire, which needs to be musically diverse as well as reflecting, in the words, a wide variety of interests (see resources). It might also be worth looking at the pitch range of the repertoire. It is possible that you, as the person who chooses the songs, are choosing songs which suit your voice (so that you are comfortable singing them) and forgetting the vocal range of the children. Most song books for children are mindful of this, but when singing unaccompanied it is worth experimenting by starting a song one degree in pitch lower (or higher) to see if it suits the children's voices better.

Singing is a physical activity, and how you stand or sit will have an effect on the quality of the sound you produce. Children spend a lot of singing time in school sitting cross-legged on the floor – probably the worst position for singing that could be devised, as the muscles that support the breathing are compressed. Teach songs and practise them standing up; this may have the effect of making singing sessions shorter, but more focused and enjoyable. It allows some ease of movement and should encourage a physical response to the music. We should sing with our whole body, not just from the neck up!

As with physical education, dance, or drama, sessions should start with a warm-up. In this way everyone has a chance to focus as a group, exercise the voice and, literally, tune in. Some stretching and relaxing exercises for the whole body, breathing, articulation, tuning, dynamic control can all be given some attention through brief, enjoyable games. They also give you a chance to assess individual children without disrupting the flow of the lesson.

ACTIVITY 3.5

In a circle, pass a 'sssh' round, then try again making the 'sssh' continuous – only stop your sound when you can hear your neighbour has started. Pass other sounds (ssssss, zzzzzzz, etc.) and when the group can do these fluently, matching each other's sounds closely, introduce a particular pitch on a hum. To begin with there will be some variation, and do not be critical of those who don't match it. Repetition, every now and then, of the original note will help. Gradually you can suggest refinement: seamless sound, consistent dynamic level, gradually getting louder or quieter.

With more experienced singers (Years 5 and 6) sing/hum one note and ask them to pass it on; everyone keeps sounding until you introduce another note, and so on. In this way note clusters or chords will emerge. This is quite demanding and will help to develop and to assess the ability to sing in parts.

The same activity can be done using rhythm patterns.

Controlling pitch

ACTIVITY 3.6

Playing with pitch helps to give flexibility and control. The conductor stretches out her arm straight in front with her hand in a fist. Everyone finds a note to hum in the middle of their range (it doesn't have to be the same as everyone else). As the conductor raises or lowers her arm, the hums get higher or lower; the middle position should represent the 'home' note.

If the arm is still, then the hum stays on one note. Opening the hand could change the hum to an 'aaah'. Use two conductors (or both arms) to conduct two sub-groups. The voices should slide rather than step. At KS1 a less abstract version can be used by drawing a mountainous outline on the board or on paper. Use a toy (doll, tractor, animal, etc.) to climb up and down the mountains (include some plateaux). The children imitate the movement with their voices. Children can then invent (compose) their own landscapes and perform them individually or in groups.

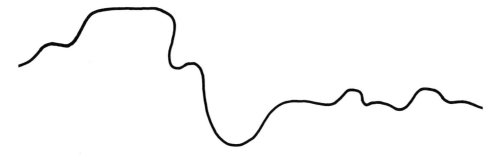

This idea can be transferred to instruments such as the slide or swanee whistle, xylophones (played by rubbing the beater up and down, rather than articulating each note), violin and cello (sliding fingers on the strings), pitch bending on an electronic keyboard, and the trombone, of course!

 ACTIVITY 3.7

To develop this idea, outline a horizontal rather than a vertical pitch contour with your hand (or whole body movement) and ask the group to follow the ups and downs with their voices (as described above).

Then ask them to look at the shape first, remember it, and perform the shape from memory. This could be explored independently in pairs or small groups: singing body shapes, contours of a landscape or skyline (like the suggestion for KS1 above), a skipping rope laid out on the floor. If there are two lines, you have two-part music.

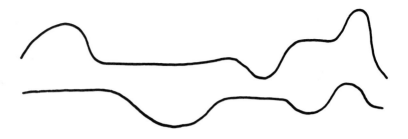

Singing can be the vehicle for all kinds of learning in music. In the classroom an informal and unthreatening environment can be provided for nurturing confidence, experimentation and quality. For most of the their time in school, children will have very little opportunity to hear their own singing voice on its own. If you cannot hear your own voice, pitching is impossible, so if solo singing becomes a natural part of performing there is more likelihood of accuracy and quality developing. It also allows you to assess children's singing as part of normal activity. Game-songs in which individuals have to sing a response or improvise words are invaluable.

Simple question-and-answer songs on two notes (the ones we use when we call, e.g. G and E), and singing the register are well-used strategies to build confidence and strength in the voice. Some children will need support from you, or one or two other children, at first. Don't insist on solo singing from everyone straight away, nor should you need to draw attention to poor tuning. Repetition and your praise and encouragement should work in time.

Singing into a real or pretend microphone (karaoke style) can have a marked effect on overcoming inhibitions!

MELODY

In *Ear Cleaning* (1967), R. Murray Schafer writes that 'A melody . . . is like taking a tone for a walk'; children need to be taken on such walks – and to go alone, use a map – and invent their own, to follow well-trodden paths – and unfamiliar ones.

So far, I have focused on pitch as a physical element of sound. Melody is the result of organising pitched sounds into patterns. Different styles and traditions apply different 'rules' as to how the pitches relate to each other, and this is where scales and modes appear. First let us invent our own rules.

ACTIVITY 3.8

In a circle give everyone a tuned, ringing sound (chime bar, hand chime, Indian bells, triangle). Choice of pitch and position in the circle should be entirely random – just make sure beforehand that there is a fairly wide range of pitch represented. Practise playing round the circle making one sound each, aiming for a regular, slowish pulse, and an even dynamic.

Building a melody

When this is achieved (after two or three goes), ask for some suggestions for pauses in the 'chain' to give some shape. Try them out, giving every suggestion a chance to be heard. There is often a high degree of consensus, but votes could be taken to agree on the final version. Through the repetition of the chain we start to make sense of it, turning it into music before our very ears. This kind of random composing liberates us from pre-set rules which might make us feel inhibited. Explore ways of developing the piece through repetitions of sections, reversing it, varying the speed or dynamics.

A development of this whole-class composition could be to divide into groups of about five. Using the same kind of random selection of pitches, compose a musical clock chime (carillon, or musical box tune) and finish by striking three o'clock. If the chime is complicated or quite long, it might be helpful to write it down. Individual children might then go on to compose their own piece on paper for others to play (the need for clarity in the chosen notation then becomes important).

Many twentieth-century composers have abandoned familiar rules or invented new ones. This is, perhaps, one of the reasons many people find much modern 'serious' music so hard to understand and appreciate. Investigating, using and inventing musical rules will help our understanding and enjoyment of a broad and diverse repertoire.

Modes and scales provide a framework in which melodies (and harmony) are composed. We unconsciously absorb the rules of major and minor scales so well that we are unnerved when they are broken.

To ensure some success when working with a whole class it is a good idea to limit the scale or mode. Throughout KS1 and 2, children should have the opportunity to compose using several different ones: familiar, unfamiliar and newly invented.

ACTIVITY 3.9

Use tuned percussion or keyboards and other instruments that children are learning (such as recorder, violin, flute, keyboard) if space and acoustics allow.

You could begin with as few as two notes (as above, in the G–E songs), but for the purposes of this example choose three adjacent notes (e.g. CDE, GAB, DEF, etc.). If using keyboards you can see how the steps (intervals) between the notes vary (compare CDE to DEF). Your choice of notes may be partly dictated by what is available, and if you choose, say, CDE, two children can share one xylophone quite comfortably, each with their own set of notes. Try to give every child a pair of beaters and encourage them to use both.

Begin with a simple listening and performing exercise with everyone echoing short melodic patterns together, e.g.

	•	•	•	•	•	•	•	•
	E	D	C	D	,EE	D	C	
or	C	E	C	E	, D	ED	C	

Children could volunteer to give the pattern, or you might need to provide some examples initially. Vary this so that solo responses can be given. Singing the patterns could be incorporated, and encourage aural rather than visual recognition or, for this same purpose, hide the playing of the pattern (face away or behind a screen).

Invent some rhythmic phrases based on words (as in Activity 2.6) and invite the children to play the phrase as a little tune.

This is easier than just playing a string of notes all the same length, as there is more 'character' to the pattern. At this stage, with inexperienced children most of their attention will be on the mechanics of the activity and not on the musical outcomes. Gradually, as coordination and control increase, they will become more conscious of, and interested in, their composing. They may also become aware that the first (lowest) note of the three becomes more dominant and that it is the note which often ends the tune. In most scales the lowest or first note, sometimes called the 'key note', is heard as the home note. This note is the one most likely to be used for a drone in an accompaniment.

Progress through groups of notes which gradually increase and vary the melodic possibilities, e.g. CEG, CDEG, DEFGA, CDEGA. This last row of notes is an example of a pentatonic scale (five tones), which is widely used in musical traditions all over the world, including folk music in Scotland, Hungary and the USA, and both the traditional and classical musics of Indonesia (gamelan) and China.

If you play the scale several times, you should begin to hear the pattern of sound. Try starting on a different note and work out what the other notes need to be to produce the same-sounding pattern. Using a keyboard will enable you to see the patterns as well as hear them. Pentatonic scales offer a fruitful and flexible means of composing singable tunes and introducing simple harmonic accompaniments. Carl Orff exploited them as a means of developing improvisation and composing skills, and it is his influence which is still observable in much of the repertoire and teaching materials used in schools. Its most significant feature in this context is that it allows children to improvise together and compose collectively without producing a lot of dissonance.

Children will discover all sorts of melodic ideas in this way – given the time and conditions. The difficulty in school is often the lack of exactly these two things. This is where a music corner can be very profitable, even in a Year 5 or 6 classroom. An electronic keyboard, on its own or linked to a computer, with headphones will encourage individuals to develop and refine their ideas. With a headphone splitter box, two or more can share the work.

Rhymes and poetry are an excellent way of providing structure and form for composing. The verse–chorus form is particulary valuable, as is any text which has some repetition of lines and/or a regular metre. You could also use the words of existing but unfamiliar songs (unfamiliar, to avoid influence).

Singing songs and listening to music in which the tune is the most prominent element (rather than the rhythms or harmony) will feed the imagination. When learning songs, try singing without the words (to 'lah', 'moo' or humming), so that the shape of the melody is the focus. Shape the melody with hands while singing.

When listening to a piece of music, try to focus on the instrument(s) or voice carrying the melody and draw the shape of it. Avoid music with a complex orchestral texture, as it might be difficult for children to focus on the melody alone.

Children from about six to eight years old are keen to recreate familiar music such as TV theme tunes, pop songs, etc. This should not be discouraged, as this is the way we absorb and understand musical idioms, not only as part our aural memory but also in our 'muscle' memory (the patterns of movement we develop when singing and playing). Swanwick (1988) describes this stage of musical development as the 'vernacular' mode, in which 'children have entered the first phase of conventional music-making [see pages 56–7]. Their compositions are often very predictable and show that they have absorbed musical ideas from elsewhere.'

Through this developmental stage they absorb patterns, structures and techniques which can then be incorporated and manipulated in their composing. Many people seem to get stuck at this stage and are content with learning the skills which will allow them to recreate or emulate familiar music.

Music, for most of us, seems to be dominated by the desire to recreate existing music, rather than to create our own; and most if not all music teaching in the past has been concerned with the teaching of interpretation and appreciation of music composed by others. Even if this is still a major aim of music education, it is now readily accepted that the most effective way of gaining skills, knowledge and understanding is by direct involvement and participation. It is also the way in which we discover and develop our own creative abilities.

The education of a ... musical ear begins when we start to explore the means of expression, simultaneously encountering and learning to enjoy the creations and presentations of others, which then further inspire our own efforts.

(Paynter 1992:20)

Listening

Listening is the fundamental skill necessary for experiencing music as performer, composer or audience. This fact needs to be highlighted and considered, as it is often taken for granted, rather than appreciated as a skill that can be exercised, developed and refined from the earliest stages of development.

Carers of babies and very young children quite naturally use sound as a stimulus, to calm, to entertain, etc. We sing, chant, babble, provide sound-making toys, and, of course, talk to them; filling their environment with sound, some meaningful and some apparently meaningless.

Adults often adopt exaggerated intonation when communicating with young children, usually pitched higher than usual. Why? So that the child will learn to copy the natural ups and downs of speech; to reflect and reinforce the sounds the child makes and thereby develop a dialogue. We also sing rhythmic songs, bounce, rock, and jiggle them, always accompanied by vocal sounds. For children, sound and movement are fused. Gradually the two separate and become more or less disconnected. The longer a close relationship can be maintained, the better coordinated our musical responses will be.

A common complaint of primary teachers is that children don't know how to listen. In a learning situation we need to be sure that pupils will focus on some sounds and ignore others. Children need to trust and use their ears as much as their eyes; and exercising and developing listening skills in music will, of course, enhance concentration generally. These skills include discrimination, acuity and aural memory; and we need to be able to know that the child is developing them. For children at KS1 and 2, assessment of listening skills will be based on a variety of evidence – some of it directly musical, but some using other media.

So how do we know what children hear?

- Through what they say.
- Through how they move or gesture.

- Through what they draw or write.
- Through what they perform or compose in music.

All of these demand some verbal, physical or manipulative skill, and not all children will be equally competent and confident in all of these. We need to devise activities which explore a variety of responses.

Schools are not silent places (nor are homes). We discover through listening that silence is relative and momentary. For children, silence can be oppressive – associated with authority or being alone. In music we learn to listen to it, create it and appreciate it.

 ACTIVITY 4.1

Sit in a circle. The leader holds a tambourine (the more jingles, the harder this will be) and in a quiet voice explains: 'This tambourine is asleep. How do I know it's asleep?' (Answer: 'Because it's not making any noise.') 'We're going to pass it round the circle without waking it up. If it does, try to count silently, in your head, how many times.'

The success of this depends on several factors: commitment, control, ability to coordinate the passing and taking movement. With older children you might be able to move on to more demanding variants straight away: two sounds in opposite directions; an instrument which is more sensitive to movement, like sleigh bells (wellnigh impossible!).

Use this simple idea to build on. Blindfold a volunteer who stands in the middle of the circle. As the tambourine circulates, the leader says 'Stop!' Whoever is holding the instrument taps or shakes it gently and continuously, while the blindfolded child locates and walks towards the sound source.

Always aim for success; failing will not develop their abilities or encourage their confidence. Start as simply as is needed, and then you can quickly progress when you see the response.

All children can do this – even those with some hearing loss. With these children, choose a sound you know they can hear; low-pitched, resonant sounds are often effective.

Some possible progressions are suggested:

- Have two different sounds: the listener has to find one.
- Give the sounds to children next to each other in the circle.
- Increase the number of sounds.
- Decrease contrast in timbre (two different kinds of shaker).
- Use two of the same instrument and vary the pitch (two chimebars), or the dynamic, or the speed (two tambours), or the way they are played (different types of beaters).

Be aware of individual children's abilities and tailor the level of contrast to ensure success.

Many teachers will be familiar with this kind of activity, and there are countless versions in published materials (see resources).

We need to develop in ourselves and those we teach the ability to:

- imitate, repeat and remember
- recognise differences and similarities between two or more sounds
- describe these in a shared language (technical terms)
- record what we hear using appropriate means (notations).

 ACTIVITY 4.2

Take the children on a listening walk (some environments are more productive than others, so try it yourself first). Record the sounds on a tape recorder, preferably with a separate microphone. Back in the classroom, listen to the recording and discuss the sounds. Which sounds are dominant, constant, rhythmic, high-pitched, sudden, etc? What makes a sound pleasant or unpleasant (noise)?

This is an opportunity for language development and careful listening – also for recall of location and visual associations. With older children a small group (or pairs) could lead one person blindfold on a sound journey. Alternatively, make a recording of a journey beforehand and use it as the starting point. After the discussion the children could then produce a score (as a frieze for display), recording the sounds as they occurred. A mixture of representational as well as more abstract symbols will emerge, e.g. footprints, birds, etc.

- How can different dynamics be shown (sounds in the distance and sounds close up)?
- How can high or low sounds be shown?
- Remember silence.

This score can then form the basis for some composition, recreating the sounds using instruments, voices and body percussion. With KS2 this could lead into composing a piece which expresses the contrast between the human/mechanical world, and the natural world.

This same exploratory approach can, of course, be used in the classroom using all kinds of sound-makers.

 ACTIVITY 4.3

Sit in a circle. Everyone will need a sheet of paper to draw on, and a pencil. Ask the group to fold the paper into four and then open it out; number each quarter from 1 to 4 (and 5 to 8 on the reverse if necessary).

Choose a selection of instruments, bearing in mind contrast in timbre, dynamics and resonance (e.g. bass xylophone, Indian bells, drum, claves, cymbal, guiro, shaker) and various beaters. Arrange them around you so that you can play them easily and explain to the group that you are going to play a sound or pattern of sounds on the different instruments, and they should 'draw the sound', each drawing in its own space on the paper.

The fewer guidelines you give, the more open and varied the results. There is, of course, no right answer, and they should try not to look at each other's. They can draw a picture of what the sound reminds them of, or just make marks and squiggles (graphic symbols).

Here are some suggestions:

- rub a hard beater up and down the bass xylophone a few times
- slowly and gently turn the shaker
- tap the drum steadily with a drum stick, gradually getting louder and then fading away again
- a single ting on the Indian bells
- a fast scrub on the guiro with a short, thin stick.

Each one of these invites a quite different response and can introduce the idea of writing down sound in an imaginative way. As with the sound walk, it will raise questions of what the sound does physically and how we respond and relate to it. Our perceptions are a complex mix of associative experience, physical reaction to the sound itself and cultural expectation. For instance the drum sound might produce:

or:

The results of this activity should be shared and used in subsequent work involving listening and composing. Children can develop the patterns and symbols to record and communicate, with increasing refinement, their musical ideas and responses.

There are obvious links to be made between some of what will emerge and staff notation, although it is important that these should not be forced. For instance, rising pitch is often spontaneously drawn as a hill or staircase (music in cartoons reinforces this), and staff notation does this also:

Year 2 children playing from their own notation

Many sounds sounding at once (a chord or sound cluster) may be depicted as a pile or thick vertical block, which relates closely to how a chord is shown in staff notation:

But symbols for rhythm, timbre, dynamics and speed may not always relate so obviously.

Children will appreciate the concept of notation if they are given lots of opportunities to play around with their own ideas first. What is important in developing listening skills is the way that children are able to respond to, describe, record and recall the sounds they hear with increasing discrimination, sensitivity and refinement.

Because of the fundamental importance of listening, all the activities in this book develop it. Beginning a music session with a listening 'game' will focus attention and signal a different learning mode: music demands a rather different quality of attention and response to almost all other subjects and experience. Responding to musical signals simultaneously in a group, starting and stopping together, keeping time, controlling dynamics and breathing at the same moment when singing are all skills that need to be nurtured with a degree of precision and quality which is unique. Just as we expect children to change their clothing for physical education, so we can develop the expectation that children should prepare themselves to be receptive and responsive to music.

Listening skills are integral to composing and performing activity. Difficulties with singing in tune or keeping in time are first and foremost to do with the development of listening skills and the accuracy of our physical response to what we hear. We also listen as a prime activity in experiencing, enjoying and understanding music, whether made by ourselves or by others. In the course of teaching music there is an expectation that the whole experience of music will encompass the doing and the audition in a symbiotic relationship, i.e. one in which the participants are each dependent on the other.

 ACTIVITY 4.4

Use a recording of the 'Habanera' from *Carmen* by Bizet. Play as far as the end of the first chorus section. There is a continuous, repeated rhythmic pattern accompanying the singing. Tap the pattern (two fingers in the palm of the hand), first while the music is playing, then afterwards.

Make up a word phrase that fits the pattern (e.g. 'eggs and ba-con'). Invent a way of notating it without words. The notation might show either the rhythm pattern or the pitch, or both, e.g.:

etc.

This is an example of an ostinato – a repeated rhythmic and/or melodic pattern often used to provide accompaniment to a melody.

Now listen to the melody sung first by the solo voice. Shape the rises and falls with your hand in the air as you listen.

Draw the shapes on paper. You will discover that the music is quite repetitive, so try to show this in in the drawing. Now listen to the music with the next section sung by the chorus: are they singing the same or a new idea? What is the solo voice doing?

Pick out the triangle (copy in taps what it does). Devise a graphic plan (a score) of the music. Use different colours for the solo voice, the chorus, the ostinato and the triangle.

Depending on ability, time and interest this could be pursued in some detail, or roughly sketched. If the former is chosen, then graph paper could be used to plot the vertical relationships with some accuracy.

Activity 4.5 uses the basic musical elements of this piece to provide a framework for composing.

ACTIVITY 4.5

In groups, select an instrument for the ostinato, e.g. bass xylophone, and play the pattern on these notes: D A F' A (F' means the F higher than A, rather than lower).

Using two beaters, practise a few times to make it steady and fluent. Guitar or cello (plucked) could play as well or instead.

Over this, a higher melody part can then be added: choose a glockenspiel (metal-lophone is a bit too resonant), recorder, voice, violin, flute, etc. Using notes of a scale (or mode) that covers D–D' (no sharps or flats), a tune can be improvised to go with the ostinato. Think of D as the 'home' note and suggest finishing on it. Discourage attempts to imitate the original too closely – it is the style that is important.

Finally a third part can be added to fill in the rhythmic texture; choose an untuned percussion instrument (claves, tambourine, scraper, shaker, small drum). This can provide another repeated rhythm, pattern or emphasise certain beats, e.g.:

I'd like　some ice-cream

Eggs　　and ba-con

Put together the three elements (more than one player for each element can be used, depending on resources and the ability of the children to work in groups) using this structure:

		Rhythm			
	Melody 1			Melody 2	
Ostinato	× 4	Ostinato	× 2	Ostinato	× 4

Further suggestions:

- The ostinato could be played by different instruments for each section.
- Two players could improvise together.

This structure can be expanded or redesigned; the important thing is that the less experienced the composers are, the more clear and uncomplicated the framework needs to be. Too many variables will cause confusion and frustration. If a number of groups work on their own piece, each one can be linked to the others in a continuous chain, the ostinato acting as the links.

There are a great number of skills involved in this activity:

- playing as part of an ensemble
- keeping in time
- shaping a melody within a given 'mode'
- maintaining an independent part within a piece
- making connections between the style of Bizet's music and theirs.

Try to identify other skills relating to composing and performing that are practised and developed. Share, in your own language first, then look at NC statements.

This project should take several sessions and there are many other ideas that could be explored, both in music and in other subjects:

- Listen to other extracts from *Carmen*, such as 'The March of the Toreadors', and/or learn it as a song.
- Listen to authentic Spanish music such as flamenco, The Gypsy Kings, De Falla, Albeniz, Granados, Rodriguez.
- Use the composition produced by the children as the accompaniment for a dance (tape the music so that it is easy to use).
- Take the idea of the graphic score in the initial listening activity and develop the shapes and colours as a painting.

Opera is a wonderful artform to explore with children, and ideally suited to combined arts work as it encompasses music, drama, dance and art in almost equal measure. This has been recognised by professional opera companies, most of which now have well-developed education programmes taking opera into schools. They give children a direct and practical experience of making opera, exploring particular works, working with singers and seeing performances. It is worth finding out what is available in your area from touring as well as resident companies.

In contemporary Britain we are exposed to a vast amount of music in everyday life. Much of this music is only slightly attended to and not actively chosen by us – I am referring to music in shops, leisure centres, advertising, television, radio, etc. Within the music curriculum it is important to develop more active listening behaviour which encourages the listener to respond critically. Some thought, therefore, should be given to all the music used in school, as all of it can be considered part of the music curriculum.

A singer with English Touring Opera exploring *The Magic Flute* with Year 6 children

ACTIVITY 4.6

With your colleagues, draw up a list of all the occasions in the ordinary life of the school when music is used or heard.

- How much of it is live and how much recorded?
- Who chooses it?
- Is it incidental to some other purpose?
- If it is not incidental, what is its prime aim?

This exercise might reveal a surprising amount of music going on in school and one might then ask these questions:

- **Could some of this repertoire be more varied in style?**
  Many of us, through our own education, have absorbed the idea that only certain kinds of music are suitable for school. *Peter and the Wolf, The Sorcerer's Apprentice, The Planets* suite are central to this repertoire, and are certainly valuable; but an enormous wealth of music is excluded for, I suspect, not very sound reasons.
  The music we actively choose to listen to is often a reflection of quite subjective and, perhaps, private associations of feelings and experience. We do not immediately think of it as a source of interest and enjoyment to the children we teach. Most of us do not, as a matter of course, listen to music consciously thinking about how it could be used in a music lesson. There is still the feeling amongst many teachers that rock, reggae, rap and other pop music is unsuitable and of no real musical value; and that jazz and much twentieth-century 'serious' music is probably too difficult for children to appreciate. All of this is, I feel, prejudice on our part, rather than any well-founded educational argument. It is not enough merely to replicate the narrow musical diet that most people expose themselves to; it should be central to the aims of the music curriculum that children experience music from a wide and diverse repertoire. Without it, audiences and music-makers in the future will become increasingly conservative, unimaginative and sterile. Any music is appropriate if there is a sound musical and educational reason for the choice.

- **Could some of it relate more to children's learning in music?**
  When choosing music for playing in assembly, consider pieces which exemplify elements that are being explored in music lessons, such as ostinato, particular instruments, or dynamic contrast. The music might, alternatively, be chosen for its connection with a historical period or part of the world.
  Songs chosen for performance in concerts or celebrations might include some which exploit particular musical features, such as a drone accompaniment, syncopated rhythms, dynamic contrast, etc.

- **Could children be encouraged to attend more closely to it?**
  When using music for dance or physical education, give the children an opportunity to listen first, draw attention to particular features that will be used to structure their movements: a repeated rhythm which might suggest a motif in dance, a change in speed or dynamics, regular phrase lengths (English, Irish and Scottish folk dance music tends to

have four, eight or sixteen-beat phrases which shape the dance). When composing a dance the music might directly suggest particular gestures, not just provide accompaniment to ideas relating to a theme.

Outside school, most people will use music as a background to housework, reading, socialising, driving, relaxing and exercising. All of this is valuable and important, but our experience is essentially that of consumer rather than of participant. This kind of listening does not necessarily increase our musical understanding, skills or appreciation, and in the curriculum we should be primarily concerned with these.

Music also has a powerful function in our appreciation and enjoyment of other artforms, especially dance, theatre and film. Music in a film can create tension, fear, anticipation, relaxation, humour, excitement and many other feelings. Children probably absorb more music through the television and films than through any other medium, so it is worth exploiting this experience in the classroom.

 ACTIVITY 4.7

Record a few seconds of music from several television advertisements, trying to avoid voice-over (most VCRs allow you to record sound direct onto audio cassette – if not, play the extracts with the picture blacked out.) (If you have the resources make copies of the tape so that small groups or individuals can choose their own extract – this could be a music-corner activity.) Use the extracts for a recognition quiz first, then move on to listening to how the music is composed:

- What is the dominant feature of the music (melody, rhythm, dynamics, timbre)?
- What instruments are being used?
- Does the music conjure up a particular place, time, season, mood, movement?
- Does the music suggest a particular audience?
- Produce a score of the extract.

There are many possibilities for developing this into composing and performing activity; and, of course, links to be made with media education.

The scores could be swapped round and used as the starting point for different groups to interpret and perform (the audience might try to guess which advert each 'new' piece was inspired by).

Groups could invent a completely new advertisement for a product and compose the music to accompany it.

You could limit the media used by focusing on radio rather than television; or excluding spoken words altogether.

This kind of activity makes us aware of the way music can be used in a very precise and often manipulative way to draw on associations, cultural clichés and the most direct physical and emotional responses we have to sound. The same is true of soundtracks to films, music for drama or dance. The composer is not always concerned with saying something new and radical, but is aiming to heighten and enhance the experience for the audience in the most direct way possible.

So far, recorded music and the school's own performing repertoire have been suggested as the source of listening material. It is also vital that children have as much experience of listening to others making music. This might range from performances given by groups in their own school, to visits from secondary school students, musicians in the community and professionals. Visits to operas, dance, music-theatre and concerts in conjunction with preparatory workshops or talks will broaden and deepen understanding and appreciation of music itself, as well as the physical experience of its source. Children experiencing an opera singer singing at full volume in their school hall is matchless.

Experiencing live music in a wide variety of formal and informal contexts reinforces the idea of music as a social activity for both musician and audience. Seeing the music being made, feeling the effort, tension and emotion of the performers and sharing the experience with others as audience add a dimension to our appreciation and enjoyment of music which cannot be replicated by recordings.

 Valuing music is the ultimate aim of music education ... No one can oblige anyone to value anything. But we can make sure that students become skilled and sensitive with a range of materials ... and we can demonstrate our own valuing by the way we respect and attend to the music of children and others.

(UKCMET 1993)

Form

This unit aims to look at ways in which musical ideas can be developed and combined to make a 'piece' of music. We make sense of music we hear by listening for patterns in the sounds. These patterns might be short rhythmic ideas, a broad melody, or a group of elements. We can listen for the structural detail of a melody and also the way that melody is developed and how it relates to other ideas in a whole piece of music. This applies to all kinds of music, ranging from small-scale, like a pop song, to large-scale, like a symphony. In musical styles we know well we unconsciously develop an ability to recognise and even predict the patterning. Popular music relies on this to 'catch' an audience as quickly as possible. Traditional hymn tunes are another good example of predictability; if you were brought up singing these, you are probably very quick at learning new ones because they so often follow similar chord patterns and melodic shapes. Other kinds of music often purposely disrupt, surprise and confound our musical expectations, to give new insight. You only need to listen to the music played in supermarkets to appreciate how bland the predictable can be made.

Listening, composing and performing all contribute to understanding form in music. The ability to recognise form needs guidance and exercise, although I am not convinced that repeated listening or performing alone will necessarily lead to greater understanding of what's going on in the music. Purposeful listening, in which we are encouraged to listen for particular elements or features, will certainly increase awareness and understanding. It may also change our emotional response; we can 'grow' to like something as we learn and appreciate its nature. Composing is the most thorough way to assess understanding, as it is through organising the sounds themselves that form is created. Describing verbally or visually what happens is second best.

Music can derive its structure from many different sources: dance, poetry, drama, story, shape and line, nature, and sound itself. The initial requirement is for some ordering of the sounds, and when working with a whole class the 'rules' for this order have to be clear and effective.

ACTIVITY 5.1

Ideally there needs to be one instrument/sound-maker for each child. Use only untuned percussion if possible. Sit in a circle and place three instruments on the floor in front of you: claves, a shaker and a scraper (guiro). Ask the children to close their eyes and listen to the claves played by you. You might ask for some comments about the sound: 'What does it make you think of?' Then ask them to listen again with eyes open and tap their index fingers together to copy the claves: 'Tap when I tap, stop when I stop.' Vary the speed and dynamics of the sound.

Repeat this sequence with each instrument, using different actions (shake hands for the shaker, rub up and down forearm for scraper). Then with eyes closed they have to respond with the appropriate actions to a sequence of the three sounds.

This should take only about five minutes and it is designed to focus attention and practise responding to sound signals. Now reverse the activity: give every child a tapper, shaker, or scraper (try to exclude very resonant sounds like cymbals and chime bars); make sure each child has decided which kind of sound they are making. Now they play in response to the appropriate action which you make; as before, vary the speed, and dynamics. Children may then volunteer to lead/conduct the sounds, although some may find it difficult to use all three actions in sequence. You could divide the class into the three sound groups, each with their own conductor, performing simultaneously or in turn.

In this way the music is being composed by the conductor out of simple movements though, admittedly, the outcomes may be rather mechanical and inexpressive, but this kind of activity should increase awareness and understanding of sound, silence, contrast and repetition, which are the basic elements in all music.

The following activities show how other conductor/composers can be used.

 ACTIVITY 5.2

This requires a pot of bubble-maker. You may need to include some preliminary steps if bubbles are likely to cause great excitement.

Sit in a circle and give every child an instrument (chime bars and shakers work well, but experiment with others). Explain to the class that the bubbles are the conductor. Each child should, secretly, choose a bubble and play their sound continuously until their bubble pops; their sound should stop with the pop. Play quietly but fast (tremolo) – a practice beforehand will help.

The alternative to this would be only playing a single quiet sound when your bubble pops. This needs far more control and concentration, and very young children may find this quite a challenge.

To develop this into a more extended piece the class could be divided into two groups: Group A plays the first version and Group B plays the second version. Different timbres could be used for each group, and the composition could have several contrasting or repeated sections, using two bubble-blowers! The children will come up with many variants to extend this idea.

It is always possible for the music that emerges from this kind of open-ended structure to be refined and developed. This should, as much as possible, be motivated by the children rather than directed by you. Your role should be to challenge, advise and assist in the realisation of their ideas and to encourage some critical discussion of the musical results.

ACTIVITY 5.3

This idea also provides an opportunity to create a piece from a 'natural' conductor/ composer.

Use body and vocal sounds and/or a variety of instruments. Ask the class to watch carefully as you spin a PE hoop in the middle of the circle. How does it move? Do the rhythm, speed and size of its movement change? Spin the hoop again and this time ask the children to make sounds that mimic its movement. Repeat two or three times to give opportunities for refinement and practice. Some sounds may suit a particular phase of the movement and not others; everyone should agree on when and how they contribute.

With more experienced children, try miming the setting off of the spin: they then perform their sounds to a memory of the hoop's movement. It can be quite uncanny how closely this performance conforms to the original, and it is also a valuable experience in being part of an ensemble.

Again, as in the bubble music, ways of developing this idea can be explored: two or three hoops starting at different times; different colours denoting different groups (timbres).

These kinds of activity provide experience of ordering and shaping sounds from natural and visible sources. The music that results employs many of the basic elements that are found in more sophisticated compositions. As I have already mentioned, in all music-making there need to be some organising principles or 'rules' which give a framework for musical ideas. These can be borrowed from other artforms, mathematics, the natural world or developed out of the nature of sound itself.

Many of the simplest structures that western music uses relate closely, and may derive from, poetry and dance. BINARY describes a piece of music in which there are two main musical ideas which contrast with or complement each other. TERNARY describes a piece with three sections in which, most commonly, the third section is a repeat of the first.

ACTIVITY 5.4

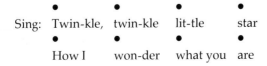

•	•	•	•
Up a-	bove the	world so	high
•	•	•	•
Like a	dia-mond	in the	sky
•	•	•	•
Twin-kle,	twin-kle	lit-tle	star
•	•	•	•
How I	won-der	what you	are

Think of each line as a musical phrase: each has the same number of beats (sing again, tapping the pulse indicated by the dots over the words).

The rhyme scheme and the repeated lines give the whole piece shape, and this is exactly reflected in the tune: there are two melodic ideas which we can call A and B. A is the tune for the first two lines and B is repeated to fit the middle two lines, then A is repeated.

This is a very slight and simple example of ternary form, which can be likened to a musical sandwich (bread-jam-bread). The B idea usually contrasts in some way with A; in this case the beginning of A jumps up while B is a descending tune.

Ternary form is widely used in all kinds of western music, from simple folk tunes to Mozart symphonies, operatic arias and jazz. There seems to be a strong need for us to be 'brought home', even when the journey is a long and complex one. Western music often describes a kind of narrative in which we are presented with the protagonists (musical ideas) who then are explored, transformed, fragmented, elaborated and developed, sometimes, it seems, beyond all recognition; before a return to familiar territory and a final re-presentation of the themes.

 ### ACTIVITY 5.5

Find other examples of this form in the familiar (school) repertoire and devise visual ways to describe them:

- Make up a dance with two different sequences of movement to go with A and B.
- Lay out a pattern of bricks (Unifix, Lego, etc.) – one colour for A one for B.
- Devise a graphic score which shows A and B as distinct.

The examples need to be quite short, which is why songs are a good place to start. (It is not always the melody which provides the contrast; it might be rhythm, dynamics, speed or texture.)

 ### ACTIVITY 5.6

Explore the idea of contrasts in sound or mood and experiment with instruments or voices.

Year 6 composing in a group

Round the circle each child improvises in turn a musical idea (this might be a single sound or a phrase) which sounds, for instance, sleepy or wide awake.

Poetry or paintings which have contrasting moods, ideas, colours or shapes can also be used.

In groups, compose a piece in sandwich (ternary) form, in which B contrasts clearly with A. The contrasts can encompass one or two elements, like loud and soft, fast and slow; or several, including timbre, number of players, melodic shape, rhythm, etc.

Alternatively, each group is either bread or jam. They work on one section and then put it together.

In this way, children develop their awareness of how music can express ideas and feelings; they also increase their ability to choose appropriate sounds and to organise, refine and perform them. With young or inexperienced children these group compositions may be rather brief and the contrasts exaggerated.

Look for ways to develop the ideas groups come up with. You need to encourage them to be critical and discriminating; and to suggest improvements or changes without becoming too heavy handed:

'What happens if you play that little tune again on a different instrument? [Quieter, slower?]'
'How about keeping that rhythm on the drum going all the time?'
'Might it be a good idea to have a silent pause (rest) before the next bit?'

Remember that, as in creative writing, children need guidance, technical advice and a certain amount of challenge to develop their skills and critical awareness. They also need lots of examples to draw on, and in music this will come not only from listening to adult music but also from listening to each other's work and talking about it.

The process of composing is not a straight path to a finished piece. It might best be described as a spiral through which the composer turns and where the turns vary in size depending on skills and experience. At any stage in the composing of a piece the composer might return to a previous stage to experiment with an idea or look for something new.

The spiral will always retain all its coils, regardless of expertise. What changes is the degree to which previous experience can slow the process down (the more possibilities, the more time spent in exploration/improvising/refining) or speed it up (the greater the expertise and knowledge, the sooner solutions are found). Craft skills speed up the process and at the

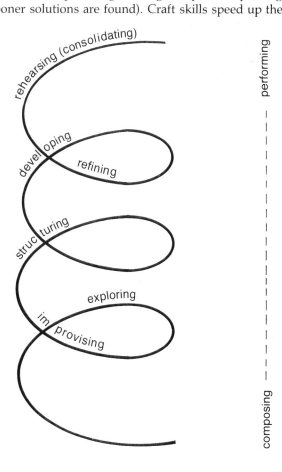

same time musical aspirations and expectations demand more time. An even moderately experienced group will settle into a composition task quickly and purposefully, for they know something of what to expect; they may also spend far more time on achieving what they want, because they have the confidence to change their minds, reject ideas and explore the musical potential of a single idea before adding something new.

Another spiral model has been proposed by Swanwick and Tillman (1986) to describe musical development in children. Their analysis of compositions collected over several years from children aged three to eleven resulted in a theory which proposes eight 'developmental modes':

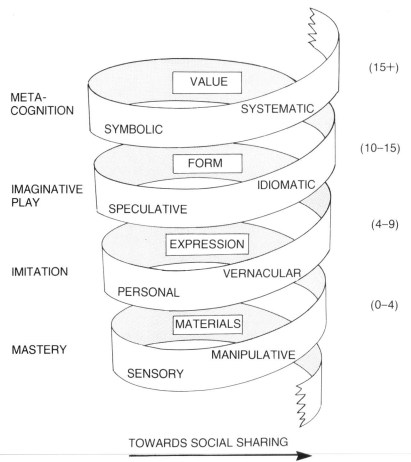

TOWARDS SOCIAL SHARING

In *Music, Mind and Education* Swanwick (1988:84–85) presents this theoretical model and its consequences for music education.

> at pre-school level, sensory exploration and the encouragement of limited manipulative control would be the main aim. In the primary school this could be taken further forward and the imitative elements of music would come more sharply into focus ... grounded in personal expression and exploration of sound but moving also towards

the acquisition of vernacular skills ... By the age of 10 or so we would be looking to further the production and recognition of musical speculation, for an understanding that all musical form depends on contrasts and repetitions and that surprises are crucial to musical structure.

It is inevitable that, as teachers learn more about what is possible and children learn to compose as a normal and continuous part of their education, this model will change; but I suspect that, for many teachers, even this model suggests a progression that has still to be realised for many of their pupils.

Music made up of contrasting and repeated sections is common in the European traditions, both folk and classical. A good example of this is RONDO form, in which the main theme (A) reappears like a chorus between contrasting sections (B,C,D ...)

 ACTIVITY 5.7

Draw a map of a journey (decide beforehand on the theme or invite the class to choose).

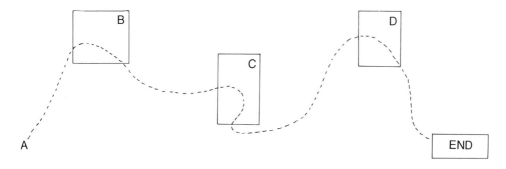

*   Who is taking the journey (creatures, humans, machines)?
*   Where are they going?
*   What happens on the way?

The map is, of course, a score, and the travellers are represented by a group who compose 'travelling' music (A) which is repeated between each event. The events (B,C,D ...) are expressed musically by different groups.

Any combinations of instruments and voices could be used, if considered appropriate. Talk about possibilities before making choices; some pre-planning for management of limited resources is essential, especially with less experienced children.

The more time is spent in exploring, listening and controlling sounds prior to such an activity, the more discriminating and musical the results.

You need to engineer some contrast between the groups: fast/slow, quiet/loud, high/low, metallic/wooden, sustained/short, etc. Each event should have a beginning, some development, and an end; and some groups may need help with this by thinking about some sort of story or sequence of 'action'. To avoid a too literal interpretation (sound effects), encourage thinking about movement, atmosphere, character and colour. Choosing a fantastic journey will also encourage imaginative outcomes: under the sea, in space, hot air balloon journey, jungle, etc. The travellers might respond to each event by varying their music. Make sure everyone knows how the journey ends (fade-out or climax?), and rehearse it separately.

When each group has rehearsed their section put the whole piece together in performance, 'conducting' with a stick which follows the path of the journey, stopping at each event. An alternative might be to have a musical 'signal' built in to the end of each travelling section (three taps on a drum, maybe), so there would be no need for a conductor.

Many versions of this idea appear in other publications, using particular topics or musical ideas (see resources). It works extremely well as a composition structure at all levels of ability. The more musically able the groups, the greater their ability will be in developing the material. Mussorgsky's *Pictures at an Exhibition* uses this same idea on a large scale; each picture is a complete piece, linked to the next by a musical promenade. This idea could be used in conjunction with children's own art work; or art work could be done in response to Mussorgsky's music. The rondo form was frequently chosen by composers of the classical period (e.g. Mozart) for final movements of concertos and symphonies.

As children learn to compose, they need to become conscious of giving structure to their ideas. Children go through a phase in their story writing in which the form of the story is a rather linear sequence of events or actions: 'I did this then I did this, then that happened', and so on. In the same way the first group compositions that they do at school tend to be a sequence of different ideas strung together. The need to organise the group itself clearly influences the structure (everyone must have a turn), but equally the experience of narrative often dominates. The facilitator of the composing process (the teacher) needs, therefore, to encourage the group to think musically rather than literally.

For a musical idea to make sense to the listener, it needs to be repeated; either exactly, or with some modification. Composing skill develops with the ability to find ways of repeating, developing, varying, transforming, and contrasting musical ideas, which may in themselves be quite small-scale. A popular type of composition amongst composers is the THEME AND VARIATIONS. This explores and demonstrates the countless ways in which a melody (theme) can be varied through manipulating one or more musical elements: speed, dynamics, articulation, rhythm, pitch, texture, timbre. There are other variables, but this list will present plenty of possibilities.

 ACTIVITY 5.8

Use the tune of *Frère Jacques* as the theme. Sing it through as a reminder, and in pairs find a way of notating it using coloured bricks and conventional or invented systems.

Notating is not absolutely necessary to this activity, but adds further opportunities for developing literacy and might help in the composing process.

In groups of about three invent two variations of it. Make sure each member of the group has an opportunity to play the original tune; begin on C if you are using xylophones etc. If you begin on a different note you will vary the melody immediately.

Depending on the experience of the participants, you might make this activity more or less prescribed:

- each variation can only change one or two elements from a list: speed, dynamics, adding notes to the tune, texture of accompaniment, rhythm, different instruments, etc.
- the 'recipe' must include a melody part, ostinato accompaniment, and a rhythm part
- the first variation must reflect a mood (sleepy, peaceful, etc.), the second, a contrast (excited, energetic, etc);
- use only voices.

After the groups have performed to each other and talked about the outcomes, play the beginning of the slow movement of Mahler's First Symphony, up to the end of the first complete playing of the melody. This is an example of how a melody can be transformed yet still be very familiar. Mahler changed it in two simple ways; listen carefully at least twice and try to sing then play his version. The trick is to start on A. The melody has the same shape, but sounds different because the intervals (distances) between the notes are altered: it is now in a minor rather than a major key.

Mahler also uses a double bass to play the tune, which contributes to the character of the music as much as the structural changes do.

The idea of taking a well-known tune and playing around with it has been popular for many centuries. In the classical repertoire there are many examples of the theme and variations form used for a complete work or as part of a larger piece such as a symphony or quartet. Composers often used it to show off their skills in a way that was easily appreciated by the audience.

Beethoven wrote many for piano, including one which uses *God Save the Queen* as the theme. Britten's *Young Person's Guide to the Orchestra,* Haydn's *Emperor* quartet (opus 76 no. 3 – slow movement) are both good examples of the form.

Looking again at *Frère Jacques,* another composing structure can be explored. This is CANON which, in its simplest version, is a ROUND. The principle is that one tune (or idea) is played by more than one part (voice or instrument) but each part starts at a different time. Very few people will have escaped the experience of *London's Burning*! The singing round is a particular kind of canon and is an accessible and enjoyable way of introducing singing and playing in parts, the concept of harmony, and canon as a musical form.

Rhythm rounds can also be explored using chanted words or body percussion.

ACTIVITY 5.9

Use a train timetable and list the names of the stations, or photocopy the whole thing (a journey from London to Aberdeen will provide great potential). Create a piece using a selection of stations which offer various rhythm patterns, e.g.:

Lon-don, Pe-ter-bo-rough, Lon-don, Pe-ter-bo-rough . . .
New-ark, New-ark, New-ark . . .
Dar-ling-ton, York, Dar-ling-ton, York . . .

Divide the class into four or five groups (the stronger their voices, the smaller the groups can be). Each group represents a train starting the journey at a different time, but following the same route, i.e. the same word rhythms. There needs to be lots of practice in performing the patterns all together before introducing the canon idea. One group could provide an ostinato made up of other words connected with trains (die-sel, lo-co-mo-tive, guard). Suggest dynamic contrast and/or changes in speed; add body percussion. Older and more confident children could compose their own piece from the timetable (see Paynter 1992). If a local journey is used, then children's knowledge of the places could add character, humour and expression to the piece (historical events, legends, geographical features, tunnels, etc.).

The idea of canon is used a great deal in dance, where the same sequence of steps or motifs is used and performed by each dancer or group one after the other.

The word 'canon' means rule, and there are two basic rules: everyone has the same material, and the timings of the entries are planned.

Maintaining independence within a piece is more demanding of listening and performing skills. If, for instance, children have to put their fingers in their ears when singing a round, then they clearly have not reached the stage where they are ready to tackle rounds musically. The joy of rounds is listening to how the parts combine and weave together. Singing in tune, keeping time and an awareness of ensemble are important requirements to performing part music. Consequently, in general, canons and rounds are most appropriate from about Year 4 onwards.

Starting points and frameworks for composing can be found outside music itself and provide strong expressive impetus. A lot of music is composed in response to or in association with other artforms – most obviously with dance. These associations are of enormous value in motivating children to compose, and provide the challenge of a 'commission' to control and refine ideas. The forms already explored above can be applied to all kinds of compositions.

Paintings can be used to suggest a mood, place, character, etc., or they can be 'read' like a graphic score. Miró, Kandinsky and Klee are all good sources for the latter. Links between Impressionist painters such as Monet, Sickert and Renoir and the music of Debussy and Ravel, which was influenced by the Impressionist movement, can enhance appreciation of both artforms.

ACTIVITY 5.10

Listen to about sixty seconds of the opening of 'Nuages' by Debussy (from the orchestral *Nocturnes*). While listening, write down any words that you feel describe the music, under these headings:

Mood   Colour   Place   Movement

Share your words with everyone; it is likely that many responses will be similar. How does the music communicate these things?

- no strong pulse or rhythm
- smooth melody line meandering and indeterminate (not one you could easily sing)
- high string sound
- quiet with some 'swells' in the dynamics

Other suggestions might be forthcoming.
      How could a similar effect be produced in the classroom?
      This kind of composing can offer the opportunity for experimentation and refinement.

Stories, descriptive prose and poetry are a rich source of ideas for composing. Formal frameworks as well as moods may be suggested. Be aware of a tendency for children to try too hard to find literal interpretations in the form of sound effects (footsteps, animal noises, etc.). Children need to explore these, but encourage them to think about mood, movement, texture, in relation to *repetition, contrast* and *silence*. Poetry is very close to music in its exploration of rhythm, speed, word sounds, structure, etc., and song is, of course, the integration of these artforms. This can be explored not only through composing songs but also by taking time when learning other songs to focus on the words and to appreciate the relationship between the words and the music.

Unit 6

Texture

The word 'texture' suggests something that can be felt, like woven cloth, and this is precisely the source of its meaning in music. Sounds can be played or sung simultaneously, travelling along together in parallel lines, or weaving in and out of each other. The lines or strands can be heard as different instruments, voices of different pitch ranges, or different rhythmic or melodic patterns.

 ACTIVITY 6.1

To continue the textile analogy, look at a piece of knitting or roughly woven cloth in which the rows are clearly visible (different colours, stitches, thickness of yarn, etc.). It might be weaving the children have produced, or the jumper you are wearing.

Choose a different vocal or instrumental sound to represent each row or band of pattern. Each player improvises a repeated rhythm or short melodic pattern for their row. This can be individual or small group work.

One player/group begins (row 1), and players join in one by one. This allows everyone to hear and appreciate each new idea.

Texture is concerned with the 'vertical' relationship between sounds and is a major element in musical style and expression. It might also be described as giving a sense of depth (a third dimension) to music.

ACTIVITY 6.2

Imagine a scene under the sea. Pictures, poems, descriptions, film, etc. could be used. There are different things going on at different depths, e.g. waving fronds of seaweed at the bottom, big slow-moving fish in the deep water, glittering shoals of tiny fish higher up, and so on.

The class can compose their own music, using layers of contrasting pitch, speed, rhythm and timbre. Devise a graphic score which clearly shows the vertical relationships between the different layers. In musical texture it is most common to find the lowest-sounding parts moving more slowly than the others. When devising this underwater composition, you might encourage this idea.

Musical texture can be 'close' and blended, like the sound of a barbershop quartet, or gospel music; it can be 'open' and unblended, where each part is distinct to the ear as in, perhaps, a small jazz group or a north Indian raga in which there is a sitar, a drone and tabla; or it can be dense and complex, like a Brahms symphony.

An open texture is much the easiest to appreciate in terms of identifying and understanding what each part is doing and how they relate. When developing a sense of texture with children, choose music which has two or three distinct voices or parts. The distinction might be in pitch, rhythm or timbre, or a combination of all three. A rich nineteenth-century symphonic sound is not an easy texture to analyse for inexperienced ears.

I have mentioned already that there are a number of ways in which musical texture is made. Simply, these are:

* combinations of pitch = harmonic texture
* combinations of rhythms
* combinations of timbre = instruments or voices

Most of the music we listen to is based on quite limited notions of harmonic texture: in popular music most songs follow similar formulae in the choice of chords; and the most familiar classical repertoire follows harmonic 'rules' that we have subconsciously absorbed as sounding 'right'. Hymn tunes and songs in the school repertoire tend to use predictable chord patterns, and it may be because of this that we are far more used to harmonic texture than to rhythmic texture, and perhaps more conservative about how we use and respond to harmony.

The way texture is used is a very important feature of different styles and traditions. Sometimes it even defines the style – as in, for instance, the blues, where the melody and structure of the song is always built on the same chord pattern. In choosing pieces of music for performing or listening, think about the general mood: energetic, calm, cheerful, restless, tense, melancholy. Then listen for how the music produces this mood: speed, rhythm, dynamics and the melodic line are the elements which are usually at the forefront of our perception. The timbre and texture may come after. This also seems to be true in developmental terms, so that in the curriculum we tend to teach first skills and understanding of those elements which communicate most immediately. This is probably a rather simplistic approach, and will certainly not apply to every piece of music, but as a general guideline it might be useful.

There are three basic ways of adding a harmonic texture to a melody: drone, ostinato, chord patterns. The first two are found in music all over the world and have a very long and respectable history in European classical music also. Medieval dance music was often accompanied by a drone bass, and some instruments have a drone built in (e.g. bagpipes, hurdy-gurdy).

The drone is a constant, fixed pitch (sometimes two pitches sounding together) which provides a 'home' note for the melody. The cello and violin, electronic keyboard or harmonium are perfect for drone playing (voices and wind players will get exhausted rather quickly). If using tuned percussion the notes need to be re-sounded, and a steady pulse should be used.

 ACTIVITY 6.3

Use tuned percussion, keyboards and any other instruments that the children are learning. In a classroom context, descant recorders and trumpets may be too dominant.

This needs to be a directed, whole-class activity first, before giving the children the opportunity to develop their own pieces.

In pairs, one plays a drone on D and the A above (middle two strings on a violin, highest two on a cello). Use the lowest range of notes that are available for the drone. The other player can then improvise using the range of notes from D up to the next D (no black notes, i.e. sharps or flats). Start with the drone holding over four beats:

```
1   2   3   4  ,1   2   3   4  ,1   2   3   4  ,1   2   3
drooooooooonnnedroooooooooonnedroooooooooonnedrooooooooo
A------------------ A------------------ A------------------ A----------
D------------------ D------------------ D------------------ D----------
```

or

```
drooooooonedronedrooooooonedronedrooooooonedronedrooooooooo
A-------------A----A-------------A----A-------------A-----A----------
D-------------D----D-------------D----D-------------D-----D----------
```

When this is settled, the partner can then join in with an improvisation, or you might suggest simply playing all the way up and down the scale a few times first to get used to the sound and practise the playing technique (encourage two beaters). Through listening to each other and experimenting, tunes will emerge and the drone player can try out different ways of articulating the drone so that it also provides a rhythmic accompaniment. Make sure everyone swaps round.

If there is a limited supply of instruments this would be very suitable as a 'music-corner' activity (ideal for two on a keyboard with headphones). Make sure there is an opportunity for everyone to hear each other's work – this could be done by recording on tape. Listen to examples of music which use drones and find a song which can be accompanied with one. Rounds are ideal, as is music based on the pentatonic scale.

Ostinato is the term used to describe a feature which arises out of the idea of a drone. The word means 'obstinate' in Italian and describes a repeated pattern (rhythmic or melodic) which creates an accompanying texture. Several patterns can be worked together, producing rich and complex textures.

ACTIVITY 6.4

Using the same resources as above, the drone part now becomes an ostinato. Make up a pattern over three beats, using D, F and A:

1	2	3	,1	2	3
D	FF	A	D	FF	A, etc.

(Combining names or words might help provide the rhythm pattern).

Over the ostinato the partner now improvises as before, but now the two parts together produce a 'busier' texture. Any number of ostinati can be added to give a multi-layered texture.

(Activities described in Unit 2 also explore rhythmic texture, and the 'Habanera' – see Activity 4.4 – uses an ostinato.)

The same idea is the basis for much of the dance music of Latin America and Africa. Each player plays an unchanging pattern which forms part of an interlocking rhythmic texture. Each part is played by a different pitch or timbre of instrument, from deep bass drums to bright, penetrating cow bells.

ACTIVITY 6.5

Lay out, for all to see, eight rectangles of blue card (bigger than playing cards). Everyone claps (clicks, slaps) the row together, in time, several times (just keeping the pulse).

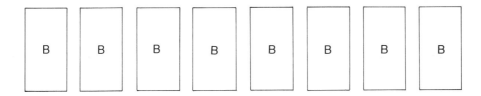

Then cover cards 1, 3 and 5 with red card of the same size.

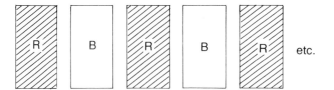

Clap the row again, clapping louder on the red. Move the reds to different positions in the row to create different patterns. Divide the class into two groups, red and blue. The blue group tap quietly and evenly all the time while the red group only sound where there are red cards. Try to avoid everyone clapping or tapping; experiment with different body or vocal sounds.

The next stage is to feel rather than sound the blue pulse and only sound the red beats. When this can be sustained steadily and accurately, divide the class into five or six groups, each with their own set of eight blue and six red cards. Each group then designs their own pattern, e.g.

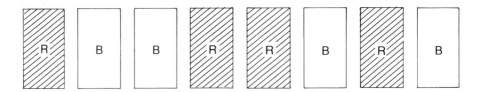

(Note that a red card on the first beat makes things a lot easier.) When each group is fluent (hear each one to check), try building a layered piece by combining the patterns. Add groups gradually so that the layers are built, one by one; someone, or one group, may need to sound the blue pulse to keep everyone together. Transfer on to percussion instruments and use this as the basis for a composition which borrows from the structure of the Brazilian samba:

Tutti (all)	Group 1	Tutti	Group 2	Tutti, etc.
×8	improvise	×4	improvise	×4

The blue pulse keeps going quietly (or internally) throughout. End with a long tutti and everyone stopping on the first beat of their pattern. An alternative (and more authentic) way of signalling the different sections would be to use a drum or samba whistle played by one player.

If it is played quite fast it will begin to sound quite Latin, but don't be too ambitious in this respect initially. The improvisation should fill four rounds of the blue pulse, i.e. 4 × 8 beats, then everyone comes straight in with the tutti.

This can provide a clear and graphic example of rhythmic texture, especially if the card patterns are lined up vertically. This way of representing rhythm is used in software packages such as RhythmBox. Using a multi-track tape recorder will also allow imaginative possibilities for 'layering' sounds.

In gamelan, the music of Bali and Java, the texture is derived from the same melodic material based on a pentatonic scale (although the tuning is very different to what we are used to). Metallophones play a cyclical melody which may be only four beats long, or much longer; lower-pitched gongs punctuate the pattern, and higher-sounding instruments play a fast, elaborated version of the melody. A drummer signals the different sections of the music, and singers, flute and string players may play over the top.

Balinese gamelan is very different to Javanese in overall sound and effect. Some of the instruments, playing techniques and musical structures are the same, but the two traditions have developed separately and distinctly. Gamelan, particularly Javanese, is becoming increasingly popular in this country, especially amongst music teachers as it enables the participation of a large group of mixed-ability players, relies on listening skills as the music is not written down, and provides a rich source of composition ideas which can be transferred to classroom instruments.

In both activities, so far, the layers have had a static quality: once introduced they are repeated many times, and do not develop or change. Western harmony has explored the way pitch combinations can transform and develop musical ideas. It is a sense of harmony which can have a powerful effect on our emotional response to music. This sense is developed through a process of acculturation: the rules of which chords to use, and in what order, developed over a period of about 300 years amongst classical composers. Despite many composers since the beginning of this century abandoning these rules, the conventions of that harmony still exert a strong influence on our listening response and on much contemporary music.

 ACTIVITY 6.6

Work with a partner, using notes C D E F G A. (Most xylophones will encompass two sets.)

On a xylophone, invent a short melody or play a familiar tune using one set of notes – something simple, played at a moderate speed.

When you can both play it, try playing together, one using the lower set of notes, the other using the higher set (you could take note B off or turn it over to mark the boundary).

Although no new notes are added, the effect is of a fuller texture. The tune is played in unison, but an octave apart. This can happen naturally when men and women sing together.

Combining different pitches together will alter the way we hear the original tune. Experiment by playing the tune with one player starting on a different note (two, three or four notes higher or lower, depending on the range of the instrument), still following the shape of the tune (parallel lines).

With two beaters each you can explore three or four note textures. The resulting sounds produce a harmonic texture. You will discover that certain combinations sound more pleasing than others. The tension and release created by moving from dissonance (clashing sounds) to consonance (pleasing sounds) is the basis of harmony and its development in European 'classical' music.

ACTIVITY 6.7

Sort out as wide a range of chime bars as you have available, including black ones. Try to include a complete run of notes from, say, low C up to the next highest C, which will give you twelve different pitches. Each player takes one bar and joins the circle. Make sure that choice and position in the circle are entirely random. Each player sounds once, steadily round the circle (check for 'duds' and a reasonable level of playing precision – tap lightly halfway along the bar, letting the bar ring and keeping the fingers of your holding hand clear). Now try making a continuous sound by repeatedly tapping the bar as fast, evenly and gently as possible. This will produce a shimmering effect (tremolo). Practise this technique with everyone playing at once, following a leader's signals for starting and stopping, loud and quiet.

The leader/composer can then invent a piece of music which explores tone clusters (groups of notes) in sequences and patterns. By pointing at individuals or sections of the circle, different clusters of sound will grow and diminish and may be shaped into a composition. Dynamics should be varied and silence used. The leader may find it easiest to imagine that her arms are the hands of a clock which can move together or independently round the circle. To use a more rhythmic structure, sections of the circle could play single clusters together and in time to a pulse, to compose a waltz, perhaps:

	1	2	3	,1	2	3	,1	2	3	,1	2	3	etc.
Group A		x	x		x	x		x	x				etc.
Group B	+			+			+						
Group C										•			etc.

Working in this way should begin to educate your ears and change perceptions of how sounds work together. There is no reason why this approach should not be used in looking at more conventional harmony. This uses three-note chords or triads which are constructed out of scales or modes. This is not the book to give a detailed account of the theory of European harmony, but a practical investigation might illuminate.

ACTIVITY 6.8

Return to your chime bar circle and remove all the black bars (replace with other white notes if possible). As a listening exercise reorganise the circle so that the pitch rises by step from the lowest note to the highest: players need to check their position against their neighbours' until the note to their left is one step lower and the note to the right one step higher. Try to ignore the letter names and sort out the scale aurally. Once accomplished, play one at a time round the circle, starting with the lowest C.

Triads are made up of alternate notes sounded together, and the three most commonly used triads in a scale are those built on the first, fourth and fifth notes (sometimes written as I, IV, V).

1	2	3	4	5	6	7	1	2	3	
C	D	E	F	G	A	B	C	D	E	etc ...
g			c	d						
e			a	b						
c			f	g						

Players can then play only in these groups (g's and c's play in two different chords).

Harmony is about relationships between sounds, so if you choose a scale other than this, which is C major, the pitches will be different, but the chords will be constructed using the same principles.

Chords made up in this way form the harmonic basis for much of our folk and popular music. It is well known amongst guitar players that you can go a long way on three chords!

ACTIVITY 6.9

Using these three chords find a familiar song with guitar chords C, F and G. Transfer the accompaniment to chime bar chords (or other tuned percussion).

Older children should be able to decide where the chords fit (harmonise) with the tune, through trial and error. Electronic keyboards will allow chords to be sustained and help to visualise the relationships between the notes of a triad.

ACTIVITY 6.10

The structure of a traditional twelve-bar blues always follows the same pattern of chords – each chord lasts for a whole bar of 4 beats:

I . . . I . . . I . . . I . . . IV . . . IV . . . I . . . I . . . V . . . IV . . . I . . . I . . .

The melody or song is improvised over this pattern.

Listen to a blues piece such as *Green Onions* by Booker T and the MGs. Can you hear when the chords change? Lay out on the floor pieces of coloured card representing each chord, e.g. red = chord I, blue = chord IV, green = chord V. Divide the class into two or three groups; each in turn dances to the music in line with the chord card and jumps to the next chord when they hear it. Some children will quickly be able to anticipate the changes, as the pattern is so regular.

Listen to other examples of both traditional blues and more 'classical' ones

('Rhapsody in Blue' by Gershwin). Traditional blues are not very appropriate for choral singing, especially in young inflexible voices, but there are many songs especially composed for children which use the blues style (see resources: song books).

Once children have absorbed something of the style and understand the chord pattern, they should be able to go on to compose their own blues. Key Stage 3 music teaching materials often include 'recipes' for this and they are certainly appropriate and relevant to Year 6.

Awareness of texture in music will develop through performing and listening to a repertoire which is varied and diverse. Group compositions will encourage this awareness, as will devising accompaniments for and arrangements of music composed by others. At KS2 it is not particularly appropriate to spend a lot of time analysing how harmony works, but children will use and appreciate harmonic texture in composing, performing and listening. It is appropriate for them to be made aware of texture in general, and to explore it freely.

Appendix 1 Relating activities to the National Curriculum (England)

In the text of this book I have deliberately made little direct reference to statements in the National Curriculum document for music. I have been concerned that teachers have the opportunity to get to grips with music itself. Through the experience and understanding gained they should then be more able to relate the National Curriculum statements to what they and their children are achieving. However, to avoid being accused of shirking my responsibility altogether, I have selected activities from the book to illustrate how they can provide evidence of attainment as described in *Music in the National Curriculum (England)* (DES 1992).

Activity	Key Stage	Attainment Target	End of KS Statement	Programme of Study
2.7	1	1	a)	i)
2.8	2	1	a) c) d)	ii) iv–vii) ix) xi) xii)
2.10	2	1	a) c)	ii) vi)
3.8	2	1	d)	x)
	2	2	b) c)	iv) v)
3.9	2	1	d)	x) xi)
4.1	1	2	a)	i)
4.2	1	2	a)	i) ii)
4.4	2	2	a) b) c)	i–iii) v)
4.5	2	1	b) c) d) e)	iv) vi–viii) xiii)

continued

Activity	Key Stage	Attainment Target	End of KS Statement	Programme of Study
5.2	2	1	b) c)	iv) ix)
5.4	1	2	a) b)	v)
5.5	1	2	a)	iii)
	1	1	d)	xi)
	2	2	e)	xiii)
5.7	1	1	a–d)	ii) iv) v) vii) viii) ix) xi)
5.10	2	2	a) c)	i) ii) v)

Appendix 2 Instruments

The sound an instrument produces is largely dependent on the quality of the instrument itself. The better the materials and craft skills that have gone into it, the better the sound, and inevitably this means that you get what you pay for. As a school, therefore, some careful decisions might have to be made.

Assemble all the instruments that the school possesses. Throw away cracked, splintered and obviously irrepairable items. Also discard instruments that have dangerously sharp edges or sound horrible.

Tuned percussion can often be much improved with an overhaul of the rubber tubing which cushions the bars. (This tubing can be obtained from shops or suppliers of school music resources.)

Remove split skins from tambourines – these can be used as jingle rings (or you can find out if they are worth repairing). After this 'purge' it will be easier to decide what is needed and where the priorities lie.

Some questions need to be considered before expanding and replacing resources:

* Which teachers and classes are going to use them?
* What range of musical activity is planned, both in and out of the classroom?
* Where does music take place?
* Will the storage need to be be static or portable?
* Who will be responsible for their maintenance?

Instruments should have a proper home to protect them and to award them the same kind of status as other equipment. There needs to be agreement about how they are stored and handled by children as well as staff; and beaters need conserving!

The following list is not exhaustive, but represents a good basic resource for primary school music-making. It takes account of pitch range and variety of timbre, as well as technical demands on players.

You will need a wide selection of beaters; as a general rule, choose felt or hard rubber for playing on wood, and plastic, felt, wood or rubber on metal. The harder the beater, the louder and brighter the sound. Don't forget drumsticks and wire brushes. For younger children, choose beaters with shorter sticks.

Tappers: claves, two-tone woodblock, tulip block, wooden agogo, castanets, temple blocks, cymbal (suspended), Indian bells, gong, metal agogo.

Scrapers: guiro, cabasa.

Shakers: marraccas, chokola, jingle stick, jingle ring, khartals, sleigh bells, rainmaker.

Drums: tambours of various sizes (tuneable and with replaceable heads), bongos, side drum on a stand, talking drum, bass drum, tambourine, tabla.

Tuned wood: soprano, alto and bass xylophones (these will come with F sharps and B flat – if you want all the 'black' notes you will need a second frame), tongue or slit drums.

Tuned metal: Soprano or alto glockenspiel, alto and bass metallophones (sharps and flats as for xylophones), chromatic octave of chime bars (C–C').

Do it yourself: all sorts of other sound-makers can be used and made. Here is a brief list of possibilities: copper piping, bunches of old keys, shells, a metal egg-slicer, walnut shells, etc.

Appendix 3 Music technology in the primary curriculum

This aspect of the music curriculum in most primary schools is underdeveloped for several reasons.

- Lack of expertise amongst music specialists and limited opportunities for in-service.
- Costs of equipment.
- Computer technology does not appear to be closely associated, in teachers' minds, with opportunities for creativity, expression and sensitivity.
- There is some evidence (Corber, Hargreaves and Colley 1993) that supports the perception that computers and related technologies have a strong masculine image and occupy the domain of male competence. It may follow that, given the predominance of female teachers in primary schools (and the feminine image of music at this phase also), there is reluctance, resistance or sheer lack of interest in the application of micro-technologies to the music curriculum. I must say that I am probably guilty of the latter, at least!
- Music in primary schools is largely seen as a collective activity and experience, whereas using a computer or other hardware seems to demand individual or small group work.
- Computer technology in schools is most exploited for its mathematical and scientific applications, as well as language-based subjects and word processing. Its use in arts teaching may not be readily considered, although there is now a diverse and imaginative range of software for visual art, but still a very limited range for music.

My own preoccupations concerning children's musical development are to do with physical and sensual expression and response to sound. A particular physical movement results in a corresponding sound: if I strike a drum with energy, the sound that results will express that energy in its dynamic; if my fingers imitate the action of rain hitting the ground, then the sound that results will be like the sound of the rain. We must ensure that children experience the physicality of sound: feel the vibrations, appreciate that the expression and dynamic of a gesture have a direct effect on what is heard.

Kemp describes this as 'body-thinking' (1990). He uses this example: 'A child with a beater in the right hand and suspended cymbal in the left, initiates a sound with a wide circular sweep of the right arm.' The movement gesture evokes an image of the sound and anticipates its quality as a result of previous experience. The difference with vocalising (which includes singing) is that the mechanisms are internal and are, of course, closely related to language. It is also important that there is an appreciation of the relationship between sound source and the sounds that can be produced. Explorations of the expressive power of the voice and the way in which the materials of the natural world are exploited to provide a vast range of musical instruments should continue to form the foundations for composing, performing and appraising.

The arguments for using microtechnology at secondary level and for those with learning difficulties have been strong and convincing. It provides a unique bridge between the performing abilities of the student and their creative ambitions. But for primary age children the arguments and applications are somewhat different.

It needs to be recognised that there are several distinct areas in which microtechnology can be applied in music:

Keyboards

Many schools have at least one keyboard, which might have been originally purchased to replace an ageing piano or to provide a portable instrument for accompanying singing. Keyboards are a resource that can have a much wider use than this. As with all equipment of this kind it is important to think about who might use it and how it will be used before buying. The design and capabilities of keyboards change rapidly and much of this is dictated by the commercial, pop music market rather than the needs of schools. Try to find some independent advice (consult other teachers, advisors and publications such as *Music Teacher*). There are, however, some basic guidelines that can be offered:

- Choose an instrument with full-sized keys and at least four octaves.
- If you want to be able to link it to a computer it must have a MIDI socket (MIDI stands for Musical Instrument Digital Interface).
- Choose a keyboard with a good range and quality of pre-set sounds and rhythms. The problem is often that virtually all the rhythms are examples of pop styles, and therefore mainly four beats in a bar. Keyboards which also allow you to make up your own rhythms, using the keyboard like a drum machine, are preferable.
- Multi-timbral keyboards will allow you to play several different sounds at once.

A keyboard which is also a synthesiser provides much greater creative opportunities, but they are expensive and its full potential might not be realised or exploited in the primary context.

Apart from its conventional functions as a portable piano, a keyboard can provide great opportunities for children to compose and perform individually or in small groups. With headphones, one or more children can develop their compositions and practise new skills without disturbing the rest of the class. Tuned percussion instruments are limited in their ability to sustain sound, and investigating harmony needs several beaters; a keyboard does this easily with one pair of hands. It will also add a range of timbres unique to the instrument which will extend the sound 'palette' for composing.

Microphones and reverb units

A reverb unit is a piece of hardware which allows you to manipulate sounds for live or recording purposes. By using different settings the resonance of a cathedral – or of a cupboard – can be added to your voice or instrument. Echo, delay and other effects which fragment and distort the sounds provided through a microphone or direct from another electronic instrument, can be produced. It is particularly effective for adding atmosphere and dramatic effects to music for drama, dance and all kinds of mixed media work.

Tape recorders

Reel-to-reel tape recorders, as well as the more fashionable four-track cassette recorders, can be exploited for music-making. Learning how to make good quality recordings of performances and compositions develops several 'strands' described in the National Curriculum (1992): communicating information, handling information, and measurement and control. It also, of course, develops listening, both in technical accuracy and through trying to achieve an effective overall sound. Multi-tracking using a four-track cassette recorder can expand the possibilities by allowing you to build, part by part, a musical texture. For example, each layer of a group composition could be recorded, one at a time, onto separate tracks and then mixed down to give a complete balanced piece. One player could record a piece involving several different instruments each playing a separate part. You could sing a four-part round with yourself!

If you use an ordinary cassette recorder, try to use an extension microphone to avoid the hiss and whirr of the machine being recorded.

Recorded sounds of all kinds – vocal and body sounds from the environment or found objects – can be used as the starting point for composing soundtracks to accompany a short video sequence or piece for radio.

Computers

There are three types of software available:

1   Grid-based composing software, such as Compose World, RhythmBox, and RhythmBed. These kinds of program enable you to compose melodies, rhythm patterns and musical texture using a variety of timbres. If you have a MIDI keyboard it may be linked to the computer, giving a greater range and quality of the sounds available.

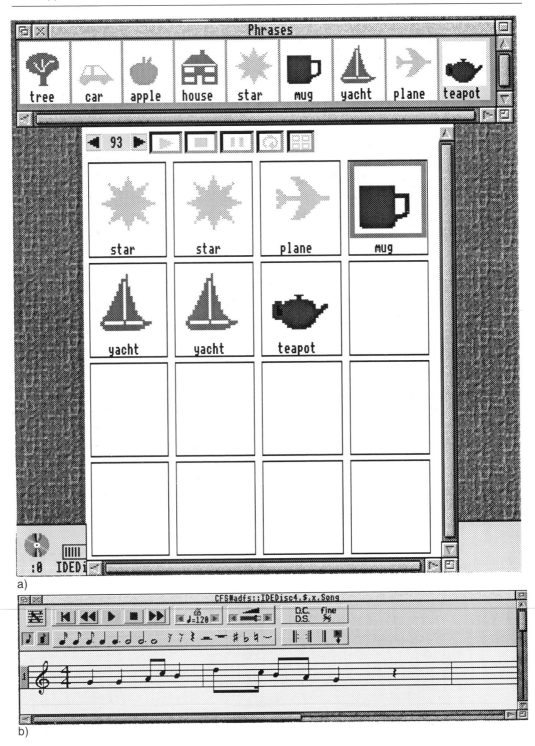

a)

b)

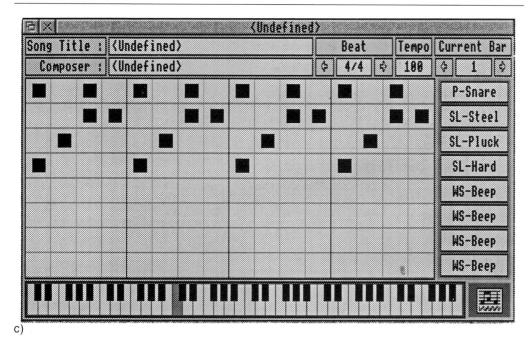

c)

a) Compose World, b) RhythmBox, c) RhythmBed

This could lead to 'sampling', a process which involves recording sounds (words, a short musical extract, found sounds, etc.) and then manipulating them in the computer. The 'sample' can be fragmented, stretched out, distorted, repeated, inverted, played backwards and so on, and can form, with other samples, a composition. Much contemporary pop music uses this process. A 'sampler' package needs to be added to the computer; this consists of a sampler board which plugs into the back of the computer and software (e.g. 'Armadeus' by Clares, 'Sound Recorder' or 'Mister Sound' by EMR).

2   Score-writing programs such as 'Notate' for composing, writing and printing out music.
3   Teaching programs for theory, performing skills and aural training.

This third category is the least relevant to the general class music curriculum, as they divorce literacy and listening skills from real musical experience, just as rudiments and theory lessons have done in the past.

With all these resources it is important to have available an amplifier, headphones and good quality speakers so that the sound reproduction is of a reasonable quality and volume.

The most important aspect to all of this is that, as far as possible, making and recording music through electronic means should be integrated with acoustic music-making and listening. Music is dependent on all kinds of technologies, ancient and modern, simple and sophisticated, 'low' and 'high'. Young children need to investigate, master and understand something of their purpose and value in the context of their own interests, needs and musical development.

Glossary of terms used

All the technical terms used are defined and usually illustrated in context. This provides a summary.

Binary Describes the form of a piece of music which has two distinct (complementary or contrasting) sections.

Canon A form of composition in which each part performs the same music but begins at different times. A **round** is a simple canon.

Chord Two or more notes of different pitches sounded together.

Consonance The blending of pitches which produce a concord.

Dissonance The 'clash' which results from certain pitches sounding together – a discord.

Dynamics The intensity of sound, which is an important means of expression in music.

Melody A sequence of notes combining both pitch and rhythm. The word 'tune' is also used, but tends to imply something fairly simple and easily identified.

Mode/scale A succession of notes, ascending or descending, which fixes the relationships between the notes and provides a 'home' note for a particular piece of music. Major and minor scales are particular modes, and although these are the most commonly used in western traditions there are many others which can still be found in European folk music, medieval music, and musics of many other cultures and traditions.

Ostinato A rhythmic or melodic pattern repeated continuously to provide an accompaniment or form part of a texture. Several different ostinati can be combined in one piece.

Phrase A sequence of notes forming a recognisable unit of melody or rhythm. In songs they correspond to the word phrases, and the singer will sing a phrase on a single breath.

Pitch The highness or lowness of a sound: a scream or the extreme right-hand notes on a keyboard have high-frequency vibrations. A rumble of thunder or a double bass have low frequency. The pitch of a sound is described in relation to others.

Pulse The regular beat felt throughout a piece of music.

Rhythm Patterns of long and short sounds which often derive from a regular pulse but may also follow a freer path, e.g. the natural rhythms of speech.

Rondo A musical form in which the main theme (A) is alternated with several contrasting sections. A might be described as a kind of chorus between verses, e.g. A B A C A.

Tempo The speed of the music's pulse.

Ternary Describes a piece with three sections, the third section usually based on the same ideas as the first (if not an exact repeat) – A B A.

Timbre The word used to describe the quality of a sound. A voice and a trumpet might produce a note of exactly the same pitch and loudness, but the timbre distinguishes them from each other.

References

Alexander, R. (1984) *Primary Teaching*, Eastbourne: Holt, Rinehart and Winston.

Corber, C., Hargreaves, D.J., Colley, A. (1993) 'Girls, boys and technology in music education', *British Journal of Music Education* 10(2) 123–134, Cambridge University Press.

DES (1992) *Music in the National Curriculum (England)*, London: HMSO.

Glover, J. (1990) 'Understanding children's musical understanding', *British Journal of Music Education* 7(3), 257–262, Cambridge University Press.

Kemp, A. (1990) 'Kinaesthesia in music and its implications for developments in microtechnology', *British Journal of Music Education* 7(3) 223–229, Cambridge University Press.

Mills, J. (1991) *Music in the Primary School*, Cambridge University Press.

Paynter, J. (1992) *Sound and Structure*, Cambridge University Press.

Schafer, M. (1967) *Ear Cleaning*, London: Universal Press.

Schafer, M. (1975) *The Rhinoceros in the Classroom*, London: Universal Edition.

Swanwick, K. (1988) *Music, Mind and Education*, London: Routledge.

Swanwick, K. and Tillman, J. (1986) 'The sequence of musical development', *British Journal of Music Education* 3(3) 305–339, Cambridge University Press.

UK Council for Music Education and Training (1993) *Guidelines on Music in the National Curriculum (England)*.

Wragg, E.C., Bennett, S.N. and Carré, C.G. (1989) 'Primary teachers and the National Curriculum', *Research Papers in Education*, Windsor: NFER Nelson.

Resources

CLASS MUSIC

Bennett, E. and Bird, W. (1989) *Music all the Time* (3 vols and cassettes), London: Chester Music.

Birkenshaw, L. (1982) *Music for Fun, Music for Learning,* Eastbourne: Holt, Rinehart and Winston.

Davies, L. (1993) *Take Note,* London: BBC.

Farmer, B. (ed.) (1982) *Springboard: Music,* London: Nelson.

Gilbert, J. and Davies, L. (1986) *Oxford Primary Music Course Stage 1,* and (1989) *Stage 2,* Oxford University Press.

Holdstock, J. (1984–8) *Earwiggo* (5 vols), Yorkshire and Humberside Association for Music in Special Education.

McNicol, R. (1992) *Sound Inventions,* Cambridge University Press.

Mary Glasgow Publications (1989–) *Music File.*

Orff-Schulwerk American Edition (1977–82): *Music for Children* (3 vols), New York: Schott.

Silver Burdett Music (3 vols) (1990), Hemel Hempstead: Simon and Schuster.

Sturman, P. (1989) *Creating Music around the World,* Harlow: Longman.

Thompson, D. and Baxter, K. (1978) *Pompaleerie Jig,* Leeds: Arnold-Wheaton.

Wishart, T. (1975) *Sounds Fun,* London: Schools Council Publications.

Wishart, T. (1977) *Sounds Fun 2,* London: Universal Edition.

York, M. (1988) *Gently into Music* (and cassette) Harlow: Longman.

CROSS-CURRICULAR AND TOPIC-BASED MATERIALS

Astles, P. and Astles, J. (1990) *Bartholomew Fair,* Oxford University Press.

Astles, P. and Astles, J. (1990) *Pilgrimage,* Oxford University Press.

Bagenal, A. and Bagenal, M. *Music from the Past* (4 vols and cassettes), Harlow: Longman.

Clarke, V. (1990) *Music through Topics,* Cambridge University Press.

East, H. (1991) *Look Lively, Rest Easy* (and cassette), London: A.&C. Black.

Gilbert, J. (1986) *Festivals,* Oxford University Press.

Gilbert, J. (1990) *Story, Song and Dance,* Cambridge University Press.

Paynter, J. and Paynter, E. (1974) *The Dance and the Drum,* London: Universal Edition.

SONG BOOKS

Ahlberg, A. and Matthews, C. (1992) *The Mrs Butler Song Book*, London: Viking.
Birkenshaw-Fleming, L. (1990) *Come on Every Body, Let's Sing*, Toronto: Thompson.
East, H. (ed.) (1989) *Singing Sack* (and cassette) London: A.&C. Black.
Gadsby, D. and Harrop, B. (1982) *Flying a Round*, London: A.&C. Black.
Rosen, M. (1992) *Sonsense Nongs*, London: A.&C. Black.
Thompson, D. and Winfield, S. (1991) *Junkanoo* (and cassette), Harlow: Longman.
Thompson, D. and Winfield, S. (1991) *Whoopsy Diddledy Dandy Dee* (and cassette), Harlow: Longman.
Tillman, J. (1983) *Kokoleoko*, London: Macmillan Education.
Tillman, J. (1985) *Mrs Macaroni*, London: Macmillan Education.

SOFTWARE

Compose (for BBC and Nimbus),
Compose World (for Archimedes), ESP.
Notate, Longman Logotron.
RhythmBox (for Archimedes), EMR.
RhythmBed (for Archimedes), Clares Micro Supplies.

MUSICIANS IN SCHOOLS

Most, if not all of the country's symphony orchestras have education programmes, as do opera and dance companies. Regional arts boards have lists of musicians who work in schools and are regionally based.

Under The Rainbow – Writers and Artists in Schools by David Morley, ed. Andy Mortimer (1991, Bloodaxe), provides an excellent guide to good practice in this field; also advice on planning, organisation and resources.

AEMS Directory of Artists for Education is a directory of artists from traditions outside Europe and North America. Available from AEMS, Commonwealth Institute, Kensington High Street, London W8 6NQ.

Index